THE POEMS OF
EDWARD THOMAS

THE POEMS OF

EDWARD THOMAS

with an introduction by PETER SACKS

HANDSEL BOOKS

an imprint of
Other Press • New York

Handsel Books gratefully acknowledges its indebtedness to Myfanwy Thomas for her gracious permission to reprint her father's verse.

Foreword copyright © 2003 Peter Sacks

Production Editor: Robert D. Hack

This book was set in 11.5 pt AGaramond by Alpha Graphics in Pittsfield, NH.

10 9 8 7 6 5 4 3 2 1

Library of Congress Cataloging-in-Publication Data

Thomas, Edward, 1878–1917.
   The poems of Edward Thomas / by Edward Thomas ; with an introduction by Peter Sacks.
      p. cm.
   ISBN 1-59051-064-X (alk. paper)
   I. Title.
   PR6039.H55A17 2003
   821'.912–dc22

                                             2003014933

CONTENTS

INTRODUCTION

God bless us all, what a thing it is to be nearing 40 & to know what one likes & know one makes mistakes & yet is right for one-self. How many things I have thought I ought to like & found reasons for liking. But now it is almost like eating apples. I don't pretend to know about pineapples and persimmons, but I know an apple when I smell it, when it makes me swallow my saliva before biting it. . . .
—letter to Gordon Bottomley

Like the apple that Edward Thomas invokes in his typically understated yet immediately vivid—almost unconsciously so—rewriting or retasting of the tree of knowledge, his poems are instantly "knowable" by their distinct savor. Indeed, many, such as "Old Man," are partly about that intimate, yet uncanny, summoning pause in which we savor what we cannot know by any other means. For Thomas, savoring was the most reliable way of at once identifying the given gists of life, and of celebrating the very ways in which distinctive objects and experiences resist our very arts of describing them. We inhale. The air is changed, scented with a material yet volatile presence that defies even as it attracts both language and consciousness. We swallow our saliva. The fruit itself remains suspended, not simply known but "saved," for that instant, in a distilled mingling of memory and anticipation. The apple literally reexerts its own power on the poet, "making" him do something involuntary. Glands, mouth, throat—not to be doubted, not to be embellished. Familiar, yet charged with something always in reserve, the apple becomes for the moment far more appetizing, even exotic, than the florid and more obviously strange pineapple or persimmon. Is it coincidental ("God bless us all") that the moment ushers in a wordless, living rejoinder to the poet's preceding sense of having made mistakes?

Apples included or aside, Edward Thomas is a poet of the perennial. Not the swagger of "make it new," but the humility, attentiveness, and open clarity of perception to "find" it so. What "it" might be—within the language and the art, within the natural world as registered by the awakened senses, memory, imagination, and, above all, within the constantly renovated affections of a human being who was neither immune from depression nor less than acutely aware of his own mortality—the following poems reveal. That they do so with such crisp lucidity, with so little inflation, with such intrinsic grace and shapeliness—this is their joy. That their clear-throated celebrations increasingly (yet obliquely, and without rancor, self-pity, or hysterical opinion) collide with an adverse historical world—the destruction of a beloved rural environment, the carnage of mass warfare in which the poet himself would be killed—this is one measure of their mature depth, their grit, their surviving claim on our attention as we turn between what might be two equally ruinous centuries.

As a poet of the perennial, Thomas formally channeled and kept clean the flow of a distinctly English plain style coursing from Chaucer to George Herbert, through early Wordsworth, John Clare, and Richard Jefferies, to Thomas Hardy—to name a few whose works he vigorously espoused in books, introductions, and reviews. Rejecting what he called the stagnant "pomp and sweetness" of late Victorian style on the one hand, and the "discord and fuss" of an overreaching, interruptive avant-garde on the other, he favored an apparently natural diction and prosody whose worn-fresh allées and fluencies have effortlessly kept pace with, if not outcoursed, the more fashionable experiments alongside. And his stylistic choices seem always to have been in service not of the poet, nor perhaps even of "poetry," but rather of those elements of a turning and returning world whose robust yet also delicate and destructible loveliness Thomas wished to witness in the deepest sense, as a communicant. Accordingly, his subjects were no more ambitious, no more intentionally (and hence obsolescently) world-historical, than his manner, as he sought out his own quietly ecstatic encounters with country lanes, birdsong, wind and rain, bright incipience of foliage, wildflowers, returning light, the various onsets of personal and historical darkness.

To bring the poems of Edward Thomas back into print, to read and especially to reread them, is therefore to pursue the poems' own primary action: the work of renewal, the uncovering of a way to perceive and to quicken the continuance of a world and of states of being that are thereby found to be not so much unprecedented—though of course his work was "revolutionary," in the sense he accorded that of his friend and colleague Robert Frost—as rather, irrepressibly, and somehow forever resurrectively, alive. Like George Herbert, but rejecting Christianity (though what authentically English poet was not also a pagan at heart?), Thomas's impulse, as he defined it wonderingly in a poem titled "Ambition," was to sing "the loveliness of prime."

From the opening "Nu" of Caedmon's hymn, or the anonymous medieval "Nu sing cuckoo," where "nu" refinds itself as both now and new, to Chaucer's inceptive "showres soote," or Clare's "I heard from morn to morn a merry thrush/Sing hymns to sunrise, and I drank the sound/With joy," or Thomas's own "glory of the beauty of the morning,—/The cuckoo crying over the untouched dew," English poets have instinctively relished what Hopkins called the "strain of the earth's sweet being in the beginning." When they recoil from a wasted world it is often either to Wordsworth's "I'd rather be a pagan," or to the Celtic mysticism that underlies the sensuously radiant reconsecrations of Vaughan or Traherne. Thomas himself, with his interest in Mabinogian tales and rural lore, was not without Druidic traces of a near-animist religion.

Admittedly, Vaughan and Traherne were Welsh, as was Thomas, whose ancestry included a Traherne. But Thomas claimed that his truest co-nationals were the birds, and his distrust of competing patriotisms, especially that of the British, included his sense that the anterior "Briton," associated with the badger of "The Combe," derived from a trans-Breton-Celtic-Gaelic stock too deep and too widely sourced for any modern nationalisms. When asked why he had volunteered for the army in July 1915, after the first crushing casualty reports had dispelled any illusions, and at the otherwise immune age of 38, he had bent down, scooped up a handful of dirt, and said, "Literally, for this." A few months later, as a soldier, he wrote, "I hate not Germans, nor grow hot/ With love of Englishmen . . . /Beside my hate for one fat patriot/ My hatred of the Kaiser is love true." If part of our unease with some of Thomas's more celebrated contemporaries rises in part from the abstractive drag of nationalist or pan-European ideologies, here again the waters of Thomas run clear. We may drink easily from his work long after other reservoirs have grown sour or in need of elaborate filtration.

———

On a loose slip of paper found inside the private diary Thomas kept during the last three months of his life, and which he was carrying in his pocket both on April 8, when he was knocked down by a shell-blast near Arras, and again on the next morning when he was killed by a shell while directing artillery fire from an exposed position, he had written three unpunctuated lines:

Where any turn may lead to Heaven

Or any corner may hide Hell

Roads shining like river up hill after rain.

In this sequence, the roads seem to survive and outshine both Heaven and Hell. They surpass either domain by sheer vivacity—

luminous, present, giving rise to figuration yet doing what even the vehicle of the river cannot do (move up hill). Perhaps purgatorial, certainly purifying in their new-washed inclinations, roads themselves were among the most recurrent objects (creatures, one might almost say) of Thomas's observation and literal transport. He was an ecstatic walker, a tramp in spirit. No other poet has written such a large proportion of poems that take the literal road, the path, the lane or track as both thematic and formal inspiration. "I love roads," begins a poem entitled "Roads," which celebrates precisely their terrestrial endurance ("Roads go on/While we forget, and are/Forgotten like a star/That shoots and is gone") even as it marks how their luster depends in part on human acts of renewal ("The hill road wet with rain/In the sun would not gleam/Like a winding stream/If we trod it not again"). When you read this alongside "Words," which speaks of a diction "Worn new/Again and again," you have a good entrée to these interanimating passages of phrasing and faring, "winding" their way between the old and the brightly recurrent.

So to read Thomas's poems is to tread a series of paths, each one distinct, each bringing the reader some unforeseen find, usually in or beyond the margin of the road, half-hidden, like the dislodged objects of "Birds' Nests," the obscured country inn of his first poem, "Up in the Wind," the hill-shrouded yard and building of "The Mountain Chapel," the marker in "The Signpost," the birdcalls, inaudible to all but the pedestrian (or the unwontedly stopped passenger) in so many signature poems. Accompanying, or rather precipitating the inscapes of a subtly unfolding journey, these finds are everywhere once glimpsed— the "white goose feathers" strewing the paths of "The Green Roads," the innumerable appeals of wildflowers, gorse, individual trees, fugitive perspectives and encounters that occur along the *way* that is a Thomas poem.

The peering sun
Sees what has been done.

The road under the trees has a border new
Of purple hue
Inside the border of bright thin grass.

Few poets match Thomas's effortless peripheral vision, essential to a sensibility so thoroughly drawn to what runs alongside our otherwise distracted linear movements. These lines from "After Rain" tell literally of border within border, while the lines rhyme across their antiphonal lengths to complicate the formal analogue for those two margins. Here, too, Thomas's predilection for what is new finds its prize in and *as* the border, just as the displacement of personal by solar vision opens up the widest margin of perception—in this case of the ephemeral but now caught-oscillating contrast of reflective light and tree-shadow. In the mind, a vast, though simply phrased track and tract have opened up from sun to bright thin grass, the last two adjectives recapitulating the range even as they lend luster to the minutely seen. To walk on through the poem is to encounter torn November leaves of hazel and thorn, burnt-orange fern, "leaflets out of the ash-tree shed/ . . . thinly spread/In the road, like little black fish, inlaid," "twelve yellow apples" (hanging, on the border between the literal and the legendary? "on one crab-tree"), and finally, with characteristic delicacy and unquenched regard for termini that suspend within themselves further initiations, "on each twig of every tree in the dell/Uncountable/Crystals both dark and bright of the rain/That begins again."

Thomas's peripheral "peerings" were magically twinned with his uncommon auditory gifts. The phrase, "A gate banged in a fence and banged in my head," opens, not least by its internal time-lag and its framed threshold between world and mind, a complex field of reflection that summons further senses to the experience of memory: "The past is the only dead thing that smells sweet,/The only sweet thing that is not also fleet," in which the reverberation of the gate, sonically alive, however mutedly, in the pursuant repetition of sounds and words, swings between closure and a persistent, fleeing openness. Not by chance, the doubled word, "sweet," tunes back in to the sensations and findings that primed the speaker's way of hearing the gate: "I heard the brook through the town gardens run./O sweet was the mud turned to dust by the sun."

Few of Thomas's poems fail to hearken especially after "things/ That we know naught of." "Hark" is the imperative that ends his first poem; my sense is that part of his desire to keep his lines acoustically clean of rhetorical fuss or clamor stemmed from his need to keep listening, well into the act of writing. His poems search out and fine-tune the frequencies of a dispersed chorus, whether of "short-lived happy-seeming things," or of enduring notes that counterpoint mere merriment. In what may be oblique acts of self-portraiture, his hearing is drawn, "over and over," by the inhuman voice of marginal, else-neglected soundings. Sweet, yes, and often bright, but seldom without a vibrant undertone, or a modulation shaken, like the owl's cry, into darker keys. Amid the "Sad songs of Autumn mirth," or the ever-farthering drift of birdsong across the shires, Thomas inevitably hears what seems to issue from a source that has an astringent power—sometimes to cheer, sometimes to edge and supplement the limits of the human will, often to chasten all self-centered human pretension or belief. Just to list the birdcalls "wisely reiterating endlessly/What no man learned yet, in or out of school" is to name a parliament, from owl to pewit, from cuckoo, thrush, chaffinch, and robin, to gull, to blackbird, and beyond, including "The Unknown Bird." This last resists all naturalists' classifications—reciprocal to solitude ("I alone could hear him. . . . Oftenest when I heard him I was alone"), as much as to the poet's ingrained, and quite modern, philosophical distrust of all systems of generalization.

Similarly, to listen to the rinsing fall, trickle, plash, silence, or gush of water in Thomas's poems is to encounter particularized instances of liquidity while having one's ears and spirit deliciously asperged. Above and around all, there is the sound of the wind, tormenting and invigorating the setting of Thomas's first poem, "Up in the Wind," preceding and outlasting the congregation's glassed-in hymns in "The Mountain Chapel" ("When Gods were young/this wind was old"), and bringing ancient music out of the "travelling air" in one of Thomas's last poems, "The Sheiling."

Acute radar or sonar may be a common attribute for lyric poets, especially those who are to be the "antennae of the race." But Thomas had a way not simply of repairing what T. S. Eliot, five years later, would follow the wartime neurologist Henry Head in calling a dissociaton of sensibility (see Thomas's "Old Man"—"I, too, often shrivel the grey shreds,/Sniff them and think and sniff again and try/Once more to think what it is I am remembering"; or "Digging [1]"—"Today I think/Only with scents"), but also of mingling his senses in complex, self-interfering variants of synesthesia. "The dim sea glints chill. The white sun is shy,/And the skeleton weeds and the never-dry,/Rough, long grasses keep white with frost" ("The Signpost"); "A train that roared along raised after it/And carried with it a mo-tionless white bower/Of purest cloud, from end to end close-knit,/So fair it touched the roar with silence" ("Ambition"); "The late year has grown fresh again and new/As Spring, and to the touch it is not more cool/Than it is warm to the gaze" ("Octo-ber"). This poet walks and writes, in other words, with a vari-ously awakened sensorium, none of whose tributary responses will be shortchanged or simplified for any dominant effect, any more than they will allow an iota of the given world to be con-ceptually abstracted without the telling measure of resistance that accrues and refines itself in the poem.

While a subtle receptiveness to all that lies at the margin of one's purview may be a crucial gift, Thomas's distinction was to suffer his gift's inseparability from a far-ranging, sensorially in-duced and felt compassion. Idiosyncratic and intellectually skep-tical by nature, he was nonetheless instinctually quick to sense what others' sense-experience might be. This gave him an alert but quiet confidence that sets him off from many of his contemporaries' struggles with subjectivism. So, too, Thomas's intuitive empathy was as much a source of his freedom as it was the very nub of that deep-rooted, unrationalizing sense of accountability that would lead him to the trenches:

Then one evening the new moon made a difference . . . At one stroke, I thought, like many other people, what things that same new moon sees eastward about the Meuse in France. Of those who could see it there, not blinded by smoke, pain or excitement, how many saw it and heeded? . . . I was deluged, in a second stroke, by another thought, or something that overpowered thought. All I can tell is it seemed to me that either I had never loved England, or I had loved it foolishly, aesthetically, like a slave, not having realised that it was not mine unless I were willing and prepared to die for it rather than leave it as Belgian women and old men and children had left their country. Something I had omitted. Something, I felt, had to be done before I could look again so composedly at English landscape, at the elms and poplars about the houses, at the purple-headed wood-betony with two pairs of leaves on a stiff stem, who stood sentinel among the grasses and bracken by hedge-side or wood's edge. What he stood sentinel for I did not know, any more than what I had got to do. . . ." ("This England")

Complacency of any kind—even of an assumed knowledge—would have imprisoned, not protected him. Comfort, he knew, was inimical to genuine acts of rejoicing. "The Owl" was written in late February 1915, three months before Thomas enlisted:

Downhill I came, hungry, and yet not starved;
Cold, yet had heat within me that was proof
Against the North wind; tired, yet so that rest
Had seemed the sweetest thing under a roof.

Then at the inn I had food, fire, and rest,
Knowing how hungry, cold, and tired was I.
All of the night was quite barred out except
An owl's cry, a most melancholy cry

Shaken out long and clear upon the hill,
No merry note, nor cause of merriment,
But one telling me plain what I escaped
And others could not, that night, as in I went.

And salted was my food, and my repose,
Salted and sobered, too, by the bird's voice
Speaking for all who lay under the stars,
Soldiers and poor, unable to rejoice.

As usual, the poet is on the road—typically aslope at that. It's hard not to take in the degree of immediate embodiment, tempered as it is by Thomas's resilient austerity and his scrupulous refusal to exaggerate. Such aspects of his bearing keep him open, in the midst of his relief, to the plain message he will hear in the owl's cry. Prolonging itself beyond the only stanza that is not end-stopped, rupturing the neat bars of the quatrains as it floats across the silent interval between words, the cry carries the poet's consciousness back outside the enclosure of the inn, and it takes over the primary act of utterance within the poem itself. Well-learned in myth and folklore though Thomas was, his actual sense-experience here enters and informs his conscience. An actual owl seems to outweigh any implicit knowledge of the bird's symbolic properties. To be moved away from what we have known toward what we sense and feel (wonderingly, suspensefully), and only thence to what we come to acknowledge; to be rescued from what comforts us to what discomfitingly claims us for the first time, or again as if for the first time—this is the reciprocal calling of "The Owl."

Few of Thomas's poems call in any other way, even when they refer to a call that is poignantly without sound. Take "In Memoriam (Easter 1915)":

The flowers left thick at nightfall in the wood
This Eastertide call into mind the men,
Now far from home, who, with their sweethearts, should
Have gathered them and will do never again.

Beyond the title's inner war between resurrective ritual time and irrevocable historical time, beyond the heart-wrenching syntax and the semantic tension of the rhymes, beyond the standoff between organic renewal and human finality, or between an erotically tender calling/culling and a brutal though discreetly off-stage cutting-short, there is of course, for us, now, the gathered knowledge of Thomas's own death, on Easter morning two years later. He had written all of his approximately 140 poems in the space of less than two and a half years.

———

Edward Thomas lies buried in a cemetery not far from where he fell, near Agny, on the outskirts of Arras. His gravestone, embedded among flowers that climb and lean between more than four hundred similar stones, is uniquely marked less by his proper name than by the single word "POET" engraved at its base. The plot is a field's breadth away from the road. At least in summer, birdsongs multiply in the surrounding trees. A visitor's book near the gate holds the names of many who have come specifically to visit this grave. Several have written out a line of his poetry, often in place of their own addresses, as if to indicate that this is where they, too, would like to be found. Several, including my immediate predecessor on the last day of June, 2002, have also recorded a sensation impossible to avoid: that of utter waste.

He was born in London on March 3, 1878. His parents had moved to the city as part of the great unmooring of rural populations during the preceding decades, but Thomas's regular visits to his grandparents, and his compulsive walking of country roads—throughout Wales and across many regions of England, especially Kent, Wiltshire, Herefordshire, Somerset, Sussex, Hampshire, Essex, and, yes, "farther and farther," Oxfordshire and Gloucestershire—kept him intimately bound to a rural, historically prior world whose days and whose acreage he knew were already more than threatened. More than from his education at St. Paul's and then at Oxford, he learned from his encounters on foot and from his precocious reading of such regional prose masters as George Borrow and Richard Jefferies. Under the mentorship of the editor James Noble, he began to write essays that would be collected in his first book, *The Woodland Life*, published when he was eighteen.

During the two decades that followed his matriculation at Oxford, Thomas kept his wife and family barely afloat on his earnings as a freelance, grindingly productive author and editor of more than forty books of prose, as well as of more than a thousand reviews. The story of his astounding turn to poetry, in late 1914, has been dominated by the account of Robert Frost's injunction: to break his existing prose into lines, bringing his inherently musical cadence and his direct speaking voice into conversation with formal prosody. Thomas himself was already well primed, having made his own careful assessments of what was wrong with the enervated artificiality of a poetry that simply couldn't give life on the page to what he valued within and around him. He championed Frost's own early work:

> *These poems are revolutionary because they lack the exaggeration of rhetoric . . . Their language is free from the poetical words and forms that are the chief material of the secondary poets. The metre avoids not only old fashioned pomp and sweetness, but the later fashion also of discord and fuss. In fact the medium is common speech . . . Mr. Frost has, in fact, gone back, as Whitman and as Wordsworth went back, through the paraphernalia of poetry into poetry once again.*

But fifteen years before this, and well before even Pound's dicta regarding what modern poetry should learn from the rigor and accuracy of good prose, Thomas had arrived at a similar position, for example in an essay titled "The Frontiers of English Prose" (1899). In an enthusiastic review of Yeats's work, he wrote, "the best lyrics seem to be the poet's natural speech," and in *How I Began*, he remembered trying to "make words of such spirit, and arrange them in such a manner, that they will *do* all that a speaker can do by innumerable gestures and their innumerable shades, by tone and pitch of voice, by speed, by pauses, by all that he was and all that he will become." In mid-1914 Thomas told Frost that he wished to make a new start as a writer, beginning with the desire to "wring the necks of my rhetoric—the geese." If this matched the state-of-the-art French campaign (Verlaine's "*Prends l'eloquence et tords-lui son cou!*"), it would not have been like Thomas to flash his sophistication, but the opening line of his first poem reads, "I could wring the old thing's neck that put it here!"—a fragment of actual speech, rather than a literary manifesto.

The poems came fast, sometimes at the rate of one a day. Within four months, Thomas had written more than fifty varied and accomplished lyrics, a pace that barely decelerated up to the last months of his life. These were not sloppy, formless outpourings, nor were they lacking in the kinds of occasion that justify a turn to poetry in the first place. Sinuous, deft, wedding speech and song in their syntactic and prosodic mastery, the poems lightly mold themselves to a shape (and often a representation of self-shaping) which they seem to hold without clutching. They move as Thomas must have walked—lithely, observantly, not wishing to disrupt the stir or shieldings of life along the edges of his path. They preserve the momentum of the stride and the swaying aftershock of the encounter. If they enter a stillness—even a stillness that knows of death—they seek out the radiating energy of that stillness: "long may it swing/ From the dead apple-bough,/So glistening."

Although they cover a mere twenty-seven months, the poems do show considerable development, both in manner and scope. To compare "November Sky" with "But These Things Also" (written less than four months later) and with "October" (after a further seven months) is to see how much more nuanced and fluent the poems became, particularly in their ability to move between inner and outer promptings, as well as in their ways of refining what might have at first seemed obvious kinds of opposition. To these shifts we can add the larger tilting, as of the poet's internal axis, as he began to absorb the visceral knowledge of the war and of his own approaching engagement as a soldier. The poems open up to a more humanly populated world, marked by suffering and by a sense of violation that cuts across Thomas's disposition to trust in a continuous life. The small masterpiece, "As the Team's Head-Brass," ends "The horses started and for the last time/I watched the clods crumble and topple over/After the ploughshare and the stumbling team." "It Was Upon," one of Thomas's sonnets written soon after enlisting, turns from a stranger's confident forecast of a good harvest to the following sestet. As often in Thomas's work, the syntax (here painstakingly hesitant in its groping resistance to the very rupture or withering it fears) carries much of the lived meaning:

> *And as an unaccomplished prophecy*
> *The stranger's words, after the interval*
> *Of a score of years, when those fields are by me*
> *Never to be recrossed, now I recall,*
> *This July eve, and question, wondering,*
> *What of the lattermath to this hoar Spring?*

Given his age, Thomas could have honorably completed the war years as a map instructor in England. But his initial decision to enlist drove him to the further choice of volunteering for the front-line artillery. During the months in France, his almost eccentric blend of stoicism and his unquenchable attentiveness to the world around him moved him to the simplest notations. February 25, 1917: "A dull morning turns sunny and warm. chaffinches and partridges, moles working on surface. . . . Does a mole ever get hit by a shell?" March 18: "Beautiful clear cloudless morning and no firing between daybreak and 8. Drew another panorama at 7. Linnets and chaffinches sing in waste trenched ground with trees and water tanks between us and Arras. Magpies over No Man's Land in pairs. The old green (grey) track crossing No Man's Land—once a country way to Arras. The water green and clear . . . with skeletons of whole trees lying there

. . . I could hear a lark till the Archies drowned it. Fired 600 rounds and got tired eyes and ears." March 21: ". . . a road between shell holes full of blood-stained water and beer bottles among barbed wire. Larks singing as they did when we went up in the dark and were shelled."

On the last page of his diary, April 8, Thomas wrote:

> The light of the new moon and every star
> And no more singing for the bird . . .
> I never understood quite what was meant by God
> The morning chill and clear hurts my skin while it delights my mind.
> Neuville in early morning with its flat straight crest with trees and houses—the beauty of this silent empty scene of no inhabitants and hid troops, but don't know why I could have cried and didn't.

The next morning, at 7:36, during the barrage against Arras, he was struck and killed by a shell.

The few poems published during Thomas's lifetime appeared under the pseudonym Edward Eastaway. He had not wanted to trade on his reputation as an established prose writer and reviewer, nor perhaps did he wish to damage it, having had numerous rejections. A collection appeared six months after his death and was followed by a sequence of editions, the most familiar of which included a moving introduction by Walter de la Mare, to whom we owe one of the most trenchant accounts of what it was like to be in Thomas's physical presence:

> But how vivid are his features in remembrance! His face was fair, long and rather narrow, and in its customary gravity wore an expression rather distant and detached. There was a glint of gold in his sun-baked hair. The eyes, long-lashed and stooping a little beneath the full rounded lids, were of a clear dark blue . . .

The lips were finely lined and wide, the chin square. His shoes were to his stature; the hands that had cradled so many wild birds' eggs, and were familiar with every flower in the Southern counties, were powerful and bony; the gestures few; the frame vigorous . . . His smile could be whimsical, stealthy, shy, ardent, mocking, or drily ironical; he seldom laughed. His voice was low and gentle, but musical, with a curious sweetness and hollowness when he sang his old Welsh songs to his children. I have never heard English used so fastidiously and yet so unaffectedly as in his talk.

Beyond the poems, Thomas is also vividly present in two books by his wife, Helen: *As It Was* (1926) and *World Without End* (1931). Their relationship was passionate, yet fraught by the poet's fierce, at times terrifyingly morose, fits of withdrawal. He would go off walking for days and nights. At times he feared his own coldness and anger. On at least one occasion, he turned against himself in an attempt at suicide. But the couple shared a remarkable candor, a capacity for instinctive delight, an almost preternatural manner of being rekindled by the beauty of the natural world. In one of the many letters exchanged between them, there is a passage that may serve to stand between this introduction and the poems. The letter is dated October 9, 1914, and was written during a long cycling trip that shortly preceded Thomas's turn to poetry:

I was first delayed by going back for my hat which I left when I was sitting. However by returning I made certain that a bird I had been hearing was the woodlark. It is a wild gentle timid song, not like a lark's so that you do not look for it up high but on trees or ground. But if you look up you see him 100 yards up making little flights and circling and hovering as if he lived there and never came down, not like the lark which soars up as high as he can get adventurously but really belongs to the earth. He stayed as long as I listened, singing all the time but with short intervals. The song is very sweet, wild and yet homely, something like a pipit's, but with a slight yodel and a smack of curlew too. As I sat there were several singing.

—Peter Sacks

Poems

Up in the Wind

"I could wring the old thing's neck that put it there!
A public-house! it may be public for birds,
Squirrels and suchlike, ghosts of charcoal-burners
And highwaymen." The wild girl laughed. "But I
Hate it since I came back from Kennington.
I gave up a good place." Her cockney accent
Made her and the house seem wilder by calling up—
Only to be subdued at once by wildness—
The idea of London there in that forest parlour,
Low and small among those towering beeches,
And the one bulging butt that's like a font.

Her eyes flashed up; she shook her hair away
From eyes and mouth, as if to shriek again;
Then sighed back to her scrubbing. While I drank
I might have mused of coaches and highwaymen,
Charcoal-burners and life that loves the wild.
For who now used these roads except myself,
A market waggon every other Wednesday,
A solitary tramp, some very fresh one
Ignorant of these eleven houseless miles,
A motorist from a distance slowing down
To taste whatever luxury he can
In having North Downs clear behind, South clear before,
And being midway between two railway lines
Far out of sight or sound of them? There are
Some houses—down the by-lanes; and a few
Are visible—when their damsons are in bloom.
But the land is wild, and there's a spirit of wildness
Much older, crying when the stone-curlew yodels
His sea and mountain cry, high up in Spring.

He nests in fields where still the gorse is free as
When all was open and common. Common 'tis named
And calls itself, because the bracken and gorse
Still hold the hedge where plough and scythe have chased
    them.
Once on a time 'tis plain that the "White Horse"
Stood merely on the border of a waste
Where horse or cart picked its own course afresh.
On all sides then, as now, paths ran to the inn;
And now a farm-track takes you from a gate.

Two roads cross, and not a house in sight
Except the "White Horse" in this clump of beeches.
It hides from either road, a field's breadth back;
And it's the trees you see, and not the house,
Both near and far, when the clump's the highest thing
And homely too upon a far horizon
To one who knows there is an inn within.

"'Twould have been different" the wild girl shrieked, "suppose
That widow had married another blacksmith and
Kept on the business. This parlour was the smithy.
If she had done, there might never have been an inn:
And I, in that case, might never have been born.
Years ago, when this was all a wood
And the smith had charcoal-burners for company,
A man from a beech-country in the shires
Came with an engine and a little boy
(To feed the engine) to cut up timber here.
It all happened years ago. The smith
Had died, his widow had set up an alehouse—
I could wring the old thing's neck for thinking of it.
Well, I suppose they fell in love, the widow
And my great-uncle that sawed up the timber:
Leastways they married. The little boy stayed on.

He was my father." She thought she'd scrub again,
—"I draw the ale and he grows fat" she muttered—
But only studied the hollows in the bricks
And chose among her thoughts in stirring silence.
The clock ticked, and the big saucepan lid
Heaved as the cabbage bubbled, and the girl
Questioned the fire and spoke: "My father, he
Took to the land. A mile of it is worth
A guinea; for by that time all the trees
Except those few about the house were gone.
That's all that's left of the forest unless you count
The bottoms of the charcoal-burners' fires—
We plough one up at times. Did you ever see
Our signboard?" No. The post and empty frame
I knew. Without them I could not have guessed
The low grey house and its one stack under trees
Was not a hermitage but a public-house.
"But can that empty frame be any use?
Now I should like to see a good white horse
Galloping on one side, being painted on the other."
"But would you like to hear it swing all night
And all day? All I ever had to thank
The wind for was for blowing the sign down.
Time after time it blew down and I could sleep.
At last they fixed it, and it took a thief
To move it, and we've never had another:
It's lying at the bottom of our pond.
But no one's moved the wood from off the hill
There at the back, although it makes a noise
When the wind blows, as if a train was running
The other side, a train that never stops
Or ends. And the linen crackles on the line
Like a woodfire rising." "But if you had the sign
You might draw company. What about Kennington?"

She bent down to her scrubbing with "Not me.
Not back to Kennington. Here I was born,
And I've a notion on these windy nights
Here I shall die. Perhaps I want to die here.
I reckon I shall stay. But I do wish
The road was nearer and the wind farther off,
Or once now and then quite still, though when I die
I'd have it blowing that I might go with it
Somewhere far off, where there are trees no more
And I could wake and not know where I was
Nor even wonder if they would roar again.
Look at those calves."

                    Between the open door
And the trees two calves were wading in the pond,
Grazing the water here and there and thinking,
Sipping and thinking, both happily, neither long.
The water wrinkled, but they sipped and thought,
As careless of the wind as it of us.
"Look at those calves. Hark at the trees again."

November

November's days are thirty:
November's earth is dirty,
Those thirty days, from first to last;
And the prettiest things on ground are the paths
With morning and evening hobnails dinted,
With foot and wing-tip overprinted
Or separately charactered,
Of little beast and little bird.
The fields are mashed by sheep, the roads
Make the worst going, the best the woods
Where dead leaves upward and downward scatter.
Few care for the mixture of earth and water,
Twig, leaf, flint, thorn,
Straw, feather, all that men scorn,
Pounded up and sodden by flood,
Condemned as mud.

But of all the months when earth is greener
Not one has clean skies that are cleaner.
Clean and clear and sweet and cold,
They shine above the earth so old,
While the after-tempest cloud
Sails over in silence though winds are loud,
Till the full moon in the east
Looks at the planet in the west
And earth is silent as it is black,
Yet not unhappy for its lack.
Up from the dirty earth men stare:
One imagines a refuge there
Above the mud, in the pure bright
Of the cloudless heavenly light:

Another loves earth and November more dearly
Because without them, he sees clearly,
The sky would be nothing more to his eye
Than he, in any case, is to the sky;
He loves even the mud whose dyes
Renounce all brightness to the skies.

March

Now I know that Spring will come again,
Perhaps tomorrow: however late I've patience
After this night following on such a day.

While still my temples ached from the cold burning
Of hail and wind, and still the primroses
Torn by the hail were covered up in it,
The sun filled earth and heaven with a great light
And a tenderness, almost warmth, where the hail dripped,
As if the mighty sun wept tears of joy.
But 'twas too late for warmth. The sunset piled
Mountains on mountains of snow and ice in the west:
Somewhere among their folds the wind was lost,
And yet 'twas cold, and though I knew that Spring
Would come again, I knew it had not come,
That it was lost, too, in those mountains cold.

What did the thrushes know? Rain, snow, sleet, hail,
Had kept them quiet as the primroses.
They had but an hour to sing. On boughs they sang,
On gates, on ground; they sang while they changed perches
And while they fought, if they remembered to fight:
So earnest were they to pack into that hour
Their unwilling hoard of song before the moon
Grew brighter than the clouds. Then 'twas no time
For singing merely. So they could keep off silence
And night, they cared not what they sang or screamed,
Whether 'twas hoarse or sweet or fierce or soft,
And to me all was sweet: they could do no wrong.
Something they knew—I also, while they sang
And after. Not till night had half its stars
And never a cloud, was I aware of silence
Rich with all that riot of songs, a silence
Saying that Spring returns, perhaps tomorrow.

Old Man

Old Man, or Lad's-love,—in the name there's nothing
To one that knows not Lad's-love, or Old Man,
The hoar-green feathery herb, almost a tree,
Growing with rosemary and lavender.
Even to one that knows it well, the names
Half decorate, half perplex, the thing it is:
At least, what that is clings not to the names
In spite of time. And yet I like the names.

The herb itself I like not, but for certain
I love it, as some day the child will love it
Who plucks a feather from the door-side bush
Whenever she goes in or out of the house.
Often she waits there, snipping the tips and shrivelling
The shreds at last on to the path, perhaps
Thinking, perhaps of nothing, till she sniffs
Her fingers and runs off. The bush is still
But half as tall as she, though it is as old;
So well she clips it. Not a word she says;
And I can only wonder how much hereafter
She will remember, with that bitter scent,
Of garden rows, and ancient damson-trees
Topping a hedge, a bent path to a door,
A low thick bush beside the door, and me
Forbidding her to pick.

               As for myself,
Where first I met the bitter scent is lost.
I, too, often shrivel the grey shreds,
Sniff them and think and sniff again and try
Once more to think what it is I am remembering,
Always in vain. I cannot like the scent,

Yet I would rather give up others more sweet,
With no meaning, than this bitter one.

I have mislaid the key. I sniff the spray
And think of nothing; I see and I hear nothing;
Yet seem, too, to be listening, lying in wait
For what I should, yet never can, remember:
No garden appears, no path, no hoar-green bush
Of Lad's-love, or Old Man, no child beside,
Neither father nor mother, nor any playmate;
Only an avenue, dark, nameless, without end.

The Signpost

The dim sea glints chill. The white sun is shy,
And the skeleton weeds and the never-dry,
Rough, long grasses keep white with frost
At the hilltop by the finger-post;
The smoke of traveller's-joy is puffed
Over hawthorn berry and hazel tuft.

I read the sign. Which way shall I go?
A voice says: You would not have doubted so
At twenty. Another voice gentle with scorn
Says: At twenty you wished you had never been born.

One hazel lost a leaf of gold
From a tuft at the tip, when the first voice told
The other he wished to know what 'twould be
To be sixty by this same post. "You shall see"
He laughed—and I had to join his laughter—
"You shall see; but either before or after,
Whatever happens, it must befall,
A mouthful of earth to remedy all
Regrets and wishes shall freely be given;
And if there be a flaw in that heaven
'Twill be freedom to wish, and your wish may be
To be here or anywhere talking to me,
No matter what the weather, on earth,
At any age between death and birth,
To see what day or night can be,
The sun and the frost, the land and the sea,
Summer, Autumn, Winter, Spring,
With a poor man of any sort, down to a king,
Standing upright out in the air
Wondering where he shall journey, O where?"

The Other

The forest ended. Glad I was
To feel the light, and hear the hum
Of bees, and smell the drying grass
And the sweet mint, because I had come
To an end of forest, and because
Here was both road and inn, the sum
Of what's not forest. But 'twas here
They asked me if I did not pass
Yesterday this way? "Not you? Queer."
"Who then? and slept here?" I felt fear.

I learnt his road and, ere they were
Sure I was I, left the dark wood
Behind, kestrel and woodpecker,
The inn in the sun, the happy mood
When first I tasted sunlight there.
I travelled fast, in hopes I should
Outrun that other. What to do
When caught, I planned not. I pursued
To prove the likeness, and, if true,
To watch until myself I knew.

I tried the inns that evening
Of a long gabled high-street grey,
Of courts and outskirts, travelling
An eager but a weary way,
In vain. He was not there. Nothing
Told me that ever till that day
Had one like me entered those doors,
Save once. That time I dared: "You may
Recall"—but never-foamless shores
Make better friends than those dull boors.

Many and many a day like this
Aimed at the unseen moving goal
And nothing found but remedies
For all desire. These made not whole;
They sowed a new desire, to kiss
Desire's self beyond control,
Desire of desire. And yet
Life stayed on within my soul.
One night in sheltering from the wet
I quite forgot I could forget.

A customer, then the landlady
Stared at me. With a kind of smile
They hesitated awkwardly:
Their silence gave me time for guile.
Had anyone called there like me,
I asked. It was quite plain the wile
Succeeded. For they poured out all.
And that was naught. Less than a mile
Beyond the inn, I could recall
He was like me in general.

He had pleased them, but I less.
I was more eager than before
To find him out and to confess,
To bore him and to let him bore.
I could not wait: children might guess
I had a purpose, something more
That made an answer indiscreet.
One girl's caution made me sore,
Too indignant even to greet
That other had we chanced to meet.

I sought then in solitude.
The wind had fallen with the night; as still
The roads lay as the ploughland rude,
Dark and naked, on the hill.
Had there been ever any feud
'Twixt earth and sky, a mighty will
Closed it: the crocketed dark trees,
A dark house, dark impossible
Cloud-towers, one star, one lamp, one peace
Held on an everlasting lease:

And all was earth's, or all was sky's;
No difference endured between
The two. A dog barked on a hidden rise;
A marshbird whistled high unseen;
The latest waking blackbird's cries
Perished upon the silence keen.
The last light filled a narrow firth
Among the clouds. I stood serene,
And with a solemn quiet mirth,
An old inhabitant of earth.

Once the name I gave to hours
Like this was melancholy, when
It was not happiness and powers
Coming like exiles home again,
And weakness quitting their bowers,
Smiled and enjoyed, far off from men,
Moments of everlastingness.
And fortunate my search was then
While what I sought, nevertheless,
That I was seeking, I did not guess.

That time was brief: once more at inn
And upon road I sought my man
Till once amid a tap-room's din
Loudly he asked for me, began
To speak, as if it had been a sin,
Of how I thought and dreamed and ran
After him thus, day after day:
He lived as one under a ban
For this: what had I got to say?
I said nothing. I slipped away.

And now I dare not follow after
Too close. I try to keep in sight,
Dreading his frown and worse his laughter.
I steal out of the wood to light;
I see the swift shoot from the rafter
By the inn door: ere I alight
I wait and hear the starlings wheeze
And nibble like ducks: I wait his flight.
He goes: I follow: no release
Until he ceases. Then I also shall cease.

After Rain

The rain of a night and a day and a night
Stops at the light
Of this pale choked day. The peering sun
Sees what has been done.
The road under the trees has a border new
Of purple hue
Inside the border of bright thin grass:
For all that has
Been left by November of leaves is torn
From hazel and thorn
And the greater trees. Throughout the copse
No dead leaf drops
On grey grass, green moss, burnt-orange fern,
At the wind's return:
The leaflets out of the ash-tree shed
Are thinly spread
In the road, like little black fish, inlaid,
As if they played.
What hangs from the myriad branches down there
So hard and bare
Is twelve yellow apples lovely to see
On one crab-tree,
And on each twig of every tree in the dell
Uncountable
Crystals both dark and bright of the rain
That begins again.

Interval

Gone the wild day.
A wilder night
Coming makes way
For brief twilight.

Where the firm soaked road
Mounts beneath pines
To the high beech wood
It almost shines.

The beeches keep
A stormy rest,
Breathing deep
Of wind from the west.

The wood is black,
With a misty steam.
Above it the rack
Breaks for one gleam.

But the woodman's cot
By the ivied trees
Awakens not
To light or breeze.

It smokes aloft
Unwavering:
It hunches soft
Under storm's wing.

It has no care
For gleam or gloom:
It stays there
While I shall roam,

Die and forget
The hill of trees,
The gleam, the wet,
This roaring peace.

Birds' Nests

The summer nests uncovered by autumn wind,
Some torn, others dislodged, all dark,
Everyone sees them: low or high in tree,
Or hedge, or single bush, they hang like a mark.

Since there's no need of eyes to see them with
I cannot help a little shame
That I missed most, even at eye's level, till
The leaves blew off and made the seeing no game.

'Tis a light pang. I like to see the nests
Still in their places, now first known,
At home and by far roads. Boys never found them,
Whatever jays or squirrels may have done.

And most I like the winter nest deep-hid
That leaves and berries fell into;
Once a dormouse dined there on hazel nuts;
And grass and goose-grass seeds found soil and grew.

The Mountain Chapel

Chapel and gravestones, old and few,
Are shrouded by a mountain fold
From sound and view
Of life. The loss of the brook's voice
Falls like a shadow. All they hear is
The eternal noise
Of wind whistling in the grass more shrill
Than aught as human as a sword,
And saying still:
"'Tis but a moment since man's birth,
And in another moment more
Man lies in earth
For ever; but I am the same
Now, and shall be, even as I was
Before he came:
Till there is nothing I shall be."

Yet there the sun shines after noon
So cheerfully
The place almost seems peopled, nor
Lacks cottage chimney, cottage hearth:
It is not more
In size than is a cottage, less
Than any other empty home
In homeliness.
It has a garden of wild flowers
And finest grass and gravestones warm
In sunshine hours
The year through. Men behind the glass
Stand once a week, singing, and drown
The whistling grass
Their ponies munch. And yet somewhere
Near or far off there's some man could

Live happy here,
Or one of the gods perhaps, were they
Not of inhuman stature dire
As poets say
Who have not seen them clearly, if
At sound of any wind of the world
In grass-blades stiff
They would not startle and shudder cold
Under the sun. When Gods were young
This wind was old.

The Manor Farm

The rock-like mud unfroze a little and rills
Ran and sparkled down each side of the road
Under the catkins wagging in the hedge.
But earth would have her sleep out, spite of the sun;
Nor did I value that thin gilding beam
More than a pretty February thing
Till I came down to the old Manor Farm,
And church and yew-tree opposite, in age
Its equals and in size. Small church, great yew,
And farmhouse slept in a Sunday silentness.
The air raised not a straw. The steep farm roof,
With tiles duskily glowing, entertained
The midday sun; and up and down the roof
White pigeons nestled. There was no sound but one.
Three cart-horses were looking over a gate
Drowsily through their forelocks, swishing their tails
Against a fly, a solitary fly.

The Winter's cheek flushed as if he had drained
Spring, Summer, and Autumn at a draught
And smiled quietly. But 'twas not Winter—
Rather a season of bliss unchangeable
Awakened from farm and church where it had lain
Safe under tile and thatch for ages since
This England, Old already, was called Merry.

An Old Song [1]

I was not apprenticed nor ever dwelt in famous Lincolnshire;
I've served one master ill and well much more than seven year;
And never took up to poaching as you shall quickly find;
But 'tis my delight of a shiny night in the season of the
year.

I roamed where nobody had a right but keepers and squires,
and there
I sought for nests, wild flowers, oak sticks, and moles, both far
and near,
And had to run from farmers, and learnt the Lincolnshire
song:
"O, 'tis my delight of a shiny night in the season of the
year."

I took those walks years after, talking with friend or dear,
Or solitary musing; but when the moon shone clear
I had no joy or sorrow that could not be expressed
By "'Tis my delight of a shiny night in the season of the
year."

Since then I've thrown away a chance to fight a gamekeeper;
And I less often trespass, and what I see or hear
Is mostly from the road or path by day: yet still I sing:
"O, 'tis my delight of a shiny night in the season of the
year."

For if I am contented, at home or anywhere,
Or if I sigh for I know not what, or my heart beats with some
fear,
It is a strange kind of delight to sing or whistle just:
"O, 'tis my delight of a shiny night in the season of the
year."

And with this melody on my lips and no one by to care,
Indoors, or out on shiny nights or dark in open air,
I am for a moment made a man that sings out of his heart:
    "O, 'tis my delight of a shiny night in the season of the
        year."

An Old Song [2]

The sun set, the wind fell, the sea
Was like a mirror shaking:
The one small wave that clapped the land
A mile-long snake of foam was making
Where tide had smoothed and wind had dried
The vacant sand.

A light divided the swollen clouds
And lay most perfectly
Like a straight narrow footbridge bright
That crossed over the sea to me;
And no one else in the whole world
Saw that same sight.

I walked elate, my bridge always
Just one step from my feet:
A robin sang, a shade in shade:
And all I did was to repeat:
    "I'll go no more a-roving
    With you, fair maid."

The sailors' song of merry loving
With dusk and sea-gull's mewing
Mixed sweet, the lewdness far outweighed
By the wild charm the chorus played:
    "I'll go no more a-roving
    With you, fair maid:
    A-roving, a-roving, since roving's been my ruin,
    I'll go no more a-roving with you, fair maid."

In Amsterdam there dwelt a maid—
Mark well what I do say—
In Amsterdam there dwelt a maid
And she was a mistress of her trade:
I'll go no more a-roving
With you, fair maid:
A-roving, a-roving, since roving's been my ruin,
I'll go no more a-roving with you, fair maid.

The Combe

The Combe was ever dark, ancient and dark.
Its mouth is stopped with bramble, thorn, and briar;
And no one scrambles over the sliding chalk
By beech and yew and perishing juniper
Down the half precipices of its sides, with roots
And rabbit holes for steps. The sun of Winter,
The moon of Summer, and all the singing birds
Except the missel-thrush that loves juniper,
Are quite shut out. But far more ancient and dark
The Combe looks since they killed the badger there,
Dug him out and gave him to the hounds,
That most ancient Briton of English beasts.

The Hollow Wood

Out in the sun the goldfinch flits
Along the thistle-tops, flits and twits
Above the hollow wood
Where birds swim like fish—
Fish that laugh and shriek—
To and fro, far below
In the pale hollow wood.

Lichen, ivy, and moss
Keep evergreen the trees
That stand half-flayed and dying,
And the dead trees on their knees
In dog's-mercury, ivy, and moss:
And the bright twit of the goldfinch drops
Down there as he flits on thistle-tops.

The New Year

He was the one man I met up in the woods
That stormy New Year's morning; and at first sight,
Fifty yards off, I could not tell how much
Of the strange tripod was a man. His body,
Bowed horizontal, was supported equally
By legs at one end, by a rake at the other:
Thus he rested, far less like a man than
His wheel-barrow in profile was like a pig.
But when I saw it was an old man bent,
At the same moment came into my mind
The games at which boys bend thus, *High-cockolorum,*
Or *Fly-the-garter,* and *Leap-frog.* At the sound
Of footsteps he began to straighten himself;
His head rolled under his cape like a tortoise's;
He took an unlit pipe out of his mouth
Politely ere I wished him "A Happy New Year,"
And with his head cast upward sideways muttered—
So far as I could hear through the trees' roar—
"Happy New Year, and may it come fastish, too,"
While I strode by and he turned to raking leaves.

The Source

All day the air triumphs with its two voices
Of wind and rain:
As loud as if in anger it rejoices,
Drowning the sound of earth
That gulps and gulps in choked endeavour vain
To swallow the rain.

Half the night, too, only the wild air speaks
With wind and rain,
Till forth the dumb source of the river breaks
And drowns the rain and wind,
Bellows like a giant bathing in mighty mirth
The triumph of earth.

The Penny Whistle

The new moon hangs like an ivory bugle
In the naked frosty blue;
And the ghylls of the forest, already blackened
By Winter, are blackened anew.

The brooks that cut up and increase the forest,
As if they had never known
The sun, are roaring with black hollow voices
Betwixt a rage and a moan.

But still the caravan-hut by the hollies
Like a kingfisher gleams between:
Round the mossed old hearths of the charcoal-burners
First primroses ask to be seen.

The charcoal-burners are black, but their linen
Blows white on the line;
And white the letter the girl is reading
Under that crescent fine;

And her brother who hides apart in a thicket,
Slowly and surely playing
On a whistle an olden nursery melody,
Says far more than I am saying.

A Private

This ploughman dead in battle slept out of doors
Many a frozen night, and merrily
Answered staid drinkers, good bedmen, and all bores:
"At Mrs. Greenland's Hawthorn Bush," said he,
"I slept." None knew which bush. Above the town,
Beyond "The Drover," a hundred spot the down
In Wiltshire. And where now at last he sleeps
More sound in France—that, too, he secret keeps.

Snow

In the gloom of whiteness,
In the great silence of snow,
A child was sighing
And bitterly saying: "Oh,
They have killed a white bird up there on her nest,
The down is fluttering from her breast."
And still it fell through that dusky brightness
On the child crying for the bird of the snow.

Adlestrop

Yes, I remember Adlestrop—
The name, because one afternoon
Of heat the express-train drew up there
Unwontedly. It was late June.

The steam hissed. Someone cleared his throat.
No one left and no one came
On the bare platform. What I saw
Was Adlestrop—only the name

And willows, willow-herb, and grass,
And meadowsweet, and haycocks dry,
No whit less still and lonely fair
Than the high cloudlets in the sky.

And for that minute a blackbird sang
Close by, and round him, mistier,
Farther and farther, all the birds
Of Oxfordshire and Gloucestershire.

Tears

It seems I have no tears left. They should have fallen—
Their ghosts, if tears have ghosts, did fall—that day
When twenty hounds streamed by me, not yet combed out
But still all equals in their rage of gladness
Upon the scent, made one, like a great dragon
In Blooming Meadow that bends towards the sun
And once bore hops: and on that other day
When I stepped out from the double-shadowed Tower
Into an April morning, stirring and sweet
And warm. Strange solitude was there and silence.
A mightier charm than any in the Tower
Possessed the courtyard. They were changing guard,
Soldiers in line, young English countrymen,
Fair-haired and ruddy, in white tunics. Drums
And fifes were playing "The British Grenadiers."
The men, the music piercing that solitude
And silence, told me truths I had not dreamed,
And have forgotten since their beauty passed.

Over the Hills

Often and often it came back again
To mind, the day I passed the horizon ridge
To a new country, the path I had to find
By half-gaps that were stiles once in the hedge,
The pack of scarlet clouds running across
The harvest evening that seemed endless then
And after, and the inn where all were kind,
All were strangers. I did not know my loss
Till one day twelve months later suddenly
I leaned upon my spade and saw it all,
Though far beyond the sky-line. It became
Almost a habit through the year for me
To lean and see it and think to do the same
Again for two days and a night. Recall
Was vain: no more could the restless brook
Ever turn back and climb the waterfall
To the lake that rests and stirs not in its nook,
As in the hollow of the collar-bone
Under the mountain's head of rush and stone.

The Lofty Sky

Today I want the sky,
The tops of the high hills,
Above the last man's house,
His hedges, and his cows,
Where, if I will, I look
Down even on sheep and rook,
And of all things that move
See buzzards only above:—
Past all trees, past furze
And thorn, where naught deters
The desire of the eye
For sky, nothing but sky.
I sicken of the woods
And all the multitudes
Of hedge-trees. They are no more
Than weeds upon this floor
Of the river of air
Leagues deep, leagues wide, where
I am like a fish that lives
In weeds and mud and gives
What's above him no thought.
I might be a tench for aught
That I can do today
Down on the wealden clay.
Even the tench has days
When he floats up and plays
Among the lily leaves
And sees the sky, or grieves
Not if he nothing sees:
While I, I know that trees
Under that lofty sky
Are weeds, fields mud, and I
Would arise and go far
To where the lilies are.

The Cuckoo

That's the cuckoo, you say. I cannot hear it.
When last I heard it I cannot recall; but I know
Too well the year when first I failed to hear it—
It was drowned by my man groaning out to his sheep "Ho!
    Ho!"

Ten times with an angry voice he shouted
"Ho! Ho!" but not in anger, for that was his way.
He died that Summer, and that is how I remember
The cuckoo calling, the children listening, and me saying,
    "Nay."

And now, as you said, "There it is" I was hearing
Not the cuckoo at all, but my man's "Ho! Ho!" instead.
And I think that even if I could lose my deafness
The cuckoo's note would be drowned by the voice of my
    dead.

Swedes

They have taken the gable from the roof of clay
On the long swede pile. They have let in the sun
To the white and gold and purple of curled fronds
Unsunned. It is a sight more tender-gorgeous
At the wood-corner where Winter moans and drips
Than when, in the Valley of the Tombs of Kings,
A boy crawls down into a Pharaoh's tomb
And, first of Christian men, beholds the mummy,
God and monkey, chariot and throne and vase,
Blue pottery, alabaster, and gold.

But dreamless long-dead Amen-hotep lies.
This is a dream of Winter, sweet as Spring.

The Unknown Bird

Three lovely notes he whistled, too soft to be heard
If others sang; but others never sang
In the great beech-wood all that May and June.
No one saw him: I alone could hear him
Though many listened. Was it but four years
Ago? or five? He never came again.
Oftenest when I heard him I was alone,
Nor could I ever make another hear.
La-la-la! he called, seeming far-off—
As if a cock crowed past the edge of the world,
As if the bird or I were in a dream.
Yet that he travelled through the trees and sometimes
Neared me, was plain, though somehow distant still
He sounded. All the proof is—I told men
What I had heard.
           I never knew a voice,
Man, beast, or bird, better than this. I told
The naturalists; but neither had they heard
Anything like the notes that did so haunt me
I had them clear by heart and have them still.
Four years, or five, have made no difference. Then
As now that La-la-la! was bodiless sweet:
Sad more than joyful it was, if I must say
That it was one or other, but if sad
'Twas sad only with joy too, too far off
For me to taste it. But I cannot tell
If truly never anything but fair
The days were when he sang, as now they seem.
This surely I know, that I who listened then,
Happy sometimes, sometimes suffering
A heavy body and a heavy heart,
Now straightway, if I think of it, become
Light as that bird wandering beyond my shore.

The Mill-Pond

The sun blazed while the thunder yet
Added a boom:
A wagtail flickered bright over
The mill-pond's gloom:

Less than the cooing in the alder
Isles of the pool
Sounded the thunder through that plunge
Of waters cool.

Scared starlings on the aspen tip
Past the black mill
Outchattered the stream and the next roar
Far on the hill.

As my feet dangling teased the foam
That slid below
A girl came out. "Take care!" she said—
Ages ago.

She startled me, standing quite close
Dressed all in white:
Ages ago I was angry till
She passed from sight.

Then the storm burst, and as I crouched
To shelter, how
Beautiful and kind, too, she seemed,
As she does now!

Man and Dog

"'Twill take some getting." "Sir, I think 'twill so."
The old man stared up at the mistletoe
That hung too high in the poplar's crest for plunder
Of any climber, though not for kissing under:
Then he went on against the north-east wind—
Straight but lame, leaning on a staff new-skinned,
Carrying a brolly, flag-basket, and old coat,—
Towards Alton, ten miles off. And he had not
Done less from Chilgrove where he pulled up docks.
'Twere best, if he had had "a money-box,"
To have waited there till the sheep cleared a field
For what a half-week's flint-picking would yield.
His mind was running on the work he had done
Since he left Christchurch in the New Forest, one
Spring in the 'seventies,—navvying on dock and line
From Southampton to Newcastle-on-Tyne,—
In 'seventy-four a year of soldiering
With the Berkshires,—hoeing and harvesting
In half the shires where corn and couch will grow.
His sons, three sons, were fighting, but the hoe
And reap-hook he liked, or anything to do with trees.
He fell once from a poplar tall as these:
The Flying Man they called him in hospital.
"If I flew now, to another world I'd fall."
He laughed and whistled to the small brown bitch
With spots of blue that hunted in the ditch.
Her foxy Welsh grandfather must have paired
Beneath him. He kept sheep in Wales and scared
Strangers, I will warrant, with his pearl eye
And trick of shrinking off as he were shy,
Then following close in silence for—for what?
"No rabbit, never fear, she ever got,
Yet always hunts. Today she nearly had one:

She would and she wouldn't. 'Twas like that. The bad one!
She's not much use, but still she's company,
Though I'm not. She goes everywhere with me.
So Alton I must reach tonight somehow:
I'll get no shakedown with that bedfellow
From farmers. Many a man sleeps worse tonight
Than I shall." "In the trenches." "Yes, that's right.
But they'll be out of that—I hope they be—
This weather, marching after the enemy."
"And so I hope. Good luck." And there I nodded
"Good night. You keep straight on." Stiffly he plodded;
And at his heels the crisp leaves scurried fast,
And the leaf-coloured robin watched. They passed,
The robin till next day, the man for good,
Together in the twilight of the wood.

Beauty

What does it mean? Tired, angry, and ill at ease,
No man, woman, or child alive could please
Me now. And yet I almost dare to laugh
Because I sit and frame an epitaph—
"Here lies all that no one loved of him
And that loved no one." Then in a trice that whim
Has wearied. But, though I am like a river
At fall of evening while it seems that never
Has the sun lighted it or warmed it, while
Cross breezes cut the surface to a file,
This heart, some fraction of me, happily
Floats through the window even now to a tree
Down in the misting, dim-lit, quiet vale,
Not like a pewit that returns to wail
For something it has lost, but like a dove
That slants unswerving to its home and love.
There I find my rest, as through the dusk air
Flies what yet lives in me: Beauty is there.

The Gypsy

A fortnight before Christmas Gypsies were everywhere:
Vans were drawn up on wastes, women trailed to the fair.
"My gentleman," said one, "You've got a lucky face."
"And you've a luckier," I thought, "if such a grace
And impudence in rags are lucky." "Give a penny
For the poor baby's sake." "Indeed I have not any
Unless you can give change for a sovereign, my dear."
"Then just half a pipeful of tobacco can you spare?"
I gave it. With that much victory she laughed content.
I should have given more, but off and away she went
With her baby and her pink sham flowers to rejoin
The rest before I could translate to its proper coin
Gratitude for her grace. And I paid nothing then,
As I pay nothing now with the dipping of my pen
For her brother's music when he drummed the tambourine
And stamped his feet, which made the workmen passing grin,
While his mouth-organ changed to a rascally Bacchanal dance
"Over the hills and far away." This and his glance
Outlasted all the fair, farmer and auctioneer,
Cheap-jack, balloon-man, drover with crooked stick, and
    steer,
Pig, turkey, goose, and duck, Christmas corpses to be.
Not even the kneeling ox had eyes like the Romany.
That night he peopled for me the hollow wooded land,
More dark and wild than stormiest heavens, that I searched
    and scanned
Like a ghost new-arrived. The gradations of the dark
Were like an underworld of death, but for the spark
In the Gypsy boy's black eyes as he played and stamped his
    tune,
"Over the hills and far away," and a crescent moon.

Ambition

Unless it was that day I never knew
Ambition. After a night of frost, before
The March sun brightened and the South-west blew,
Jackdaws began to shout and float and soar
Already, and one was racing straight and high
Alone, shouting like a black warrior
Challenges and menaces to the wide sky.
With loud long laughter then a woodpecker
Ridiculed the sadness of the owl's last cry.
And through the valley where all the folk astir
Made only plumes of pearly smoke to tower
Over dark trees and white meadows happier
Than was Elysium in that happy hour,
A train that roared along raised after it
And carried with it a motionless white bower
Of purest cloud, from end to end close-knit,
So fair it touched the roar with silence. Time
Was powerless while that lasted. I could sit
And think I had made the loveliness of prime,
Breathed its life into it and were its lord,
And no mind lived save this 'twixt clouds and rime.
Omnipotent I was, nor even deplored
That I did nothing. But the end fell like a bell:
The bower was scattered; far off the train roared.
But if this was ambition I cannot tell:
What 'twas ambition for I know not well.

House and Man

One hour: as dim he and his house now look
As a reflection in a rippling brook,
While I remember him; but first, his house.
Empty it sounded. 'Twas dark with forest boughs
That brushed the walls and made the mossy tiles
Part of the squirrel's track. In all those miles
Of forest silence and forest murmur, only
One house—"Lonely," he said, "I wish it were lonely"—
Which the trees looked upon from every side,
And that was his.

     He waved good-bye to hide
A sigh that he converted to a laugh.
He seemed to hang rather than stand there, half
Ghost-like, half a beggar's rag, clean wrung
And useless on the briar where it has hung
Long years a-washing by sun and wind and rain.
But why I call back man and house again
Is that now on a beech-tree's tip I see
As then I saw—I at the gate, and he
In the house darkness,—a magpie veering about,
A magpie like a weathercock in doubt.

Parting

The Past is a strange land, most strange.
Wind blows not there, nor does rain fall:
If they do, they cannot hurt at all.
Men of all kinds as equals range

The soundless fields and streets of it.
Pleasure and pain there have no sting,
The perished self not suffering
That lacks all blood and nerve and wit,

And is in shadow-land a shade.
Remembered joy and misery
Bring joy to the joyous equally;
Both sadden the sad. So memory made

Parting today a double pain:
First because it was parting; next
Because the ill it ended vexed
And mocked me from the Past again,

Not as what had been remedied
Had I gone on,—not that, oh no!
But as itself no longer woe;
Sighs, angry word and look and deed

Being faded: rather a kind of bliss
For there spiritualized it lay
In the perpetual yesterday
That naught can stir or stain, like this.

First Known When Lost

I never had noticed it until
'Twas gone,—the narrow copse
Where now the woodman lops
The last of the willows with his bill.

It was not more than a hedge o'ergrown.
One meadow's breadth away
I passed it day by day.
Now the soil is bare as a bone,

And black betwixt two meadows green,
Though fresh-cut faggot ends
Of hazel make some amends
With a gleam as if flowers they had been.

Strange it could have hidden so near!
And now I see as I look
That the small winding brook,
A tributary's tributary rises there.

May 23

There never was a finer day,
And never will be while May is May,—
The third, and not the last of its kind;
But though fair and clear the two behind
Seemed pursued by tempests overpast;
And the morrow with fear that it could not last
Was spoiled. Today ere the stones were warm
Five minutes of thunderstorm
Dashed it with rain, as if to secure,
By one tear, its beauty the luck to endure.

At midday then along the lane
Old Jack Noman appeared again,
Jaunty and old, crooked and tall,
And stopped and grinned at me over the wall,
With a cowslip bunch in his button-hole
And one in his cap. Who could say if his roll
Came from flints in the road, the weather, or ale?
He was welcome as the nightingale.
Not an hour of the sun had been wasted on Jack.
"I've got my Indian complexion back"
Said he. He was tanned like a harvester,
Like his short clay pipe, like the leaf and bur
That clung to his coat from last night's bed,
Like the ploughland crumbling red.
Fairer flowers were none on the earth
Than his cowslips wet with the dew of their birth,
Or fresher leaves than the cress in his basket.
"Where did they come from, Jack?" "Don't ask it,
And you'll be told no lies." "Very well:
Then I can't buy." "I don't want to sell.
Take them and these flowers, too, free.
Perhaps you have something to give me?

Wait till next time. The better the day . . .
The Lord couldn't make a better, I say;
If he could, he never has done."
So off went Jack with his roll-walk-run,
Leaving his cresses from Oakshott rill
And his cowslips from Wheatham hill.

'Twas the first day that the midges bit;
But though they bit me, I was glad of it:
Of the dust in my face, too, I was glad.
Spring could do nothing to make me sad.
Bluebells hid all the ruts in the copse.
The elm seeds lay in the road like hops,
That fine day, May the twenty-third,
The day Jack Noman disappeared.

The Barn

They should never have built a barn there, at all—
Drip, drip, drip!—under that elm tree,
Though then it was young. Now it is old
But good, not like the barn and me.

Tomorrow they cut it down. They will leave
The barn, as I shall be left, maybe.
What holds it up? 'Twould not pay to pull down.
Well, this place has no other antiquity.

No abbey or castle looks so old
As this that Job Knight built in '54,
Built to keep corn for rats and men.
Now there's fowls in the roof, pigs on the floor.

What thatch survives is dung for the grass,
The best grass on the farm. A pity the roof
Will not bear a mower to mow it. But
Only fowls have foothold enough.

Starlings used to sit there with bubbling throats
Making a spiky beard as they chattered
And whistled and kissed, with heads in air,
Till they thought of something else that mattered.

But now they cannot find a place,
Among all those holes, for a nest any more.
It's the turn of lesser things, I suppose.
Once I fancied 'twas starlings they built it for.

Home

Not the end: but there's nothing more.
Sweet Summer and Winter rude
I have loved, and friendship and love,
The crowd and solitude.

But I know them: I weary not;
But all that they mean I know.
I would go back again home
Now. Yet how should I go?

This is my grief. That land,
My home, I have never seen;
No traveller tells of it,
However far he has been.

And could I discover it,
I fear my happiness there,
Or my pain, might be dreams of return
Here, to these things that were.

Remembering ills, though slight
Yet irremediable,
Brings a worse, an impurer pang
Than remembering what was well.

No: I cannot go back,
And would not if I could.
Until blindness come, I must wait
And blink at what is not good.

The Owl

Downhill I came, hungry, and yet not starved;
Cold, yet had heat within me that was proof
Against the North wind; tired, yet so that rest
Had seemed the sweetest thing under a roof.

Then at the inn I had food, fire, and rest,
Knowing how hungry, cold, and tired was I.
All of the night was quite barred out except
An owl's cry, a most melancholy cry

Shaken out long and clear upon the hill,
No merry note, nor cause of merriment,
But one telling me plain what I escaped
And others could not, that night, as in I went.

And salted was my food, and my repose,
Salted and sobered, too, by the bird's voice
Speaking for all who lay under the stars,
Soldiers and poor, unable to rejoice.

The Child on the Cliffs

Mother, the root of this little yellow flower
Among the stones has the taste of quinine.
Things are strange today on the cliff. The sun shines so bright,
And the grasshopper works at his sewing-machine
So hard. Here's one on my hand, mother, look;
I lie so still. There's one on your book.

But I have something to tell more strange. So leave
Your book to the grasshopper, mother dear,—
Like a green knight in a dazzling market-place,—
And listen now. Can you hear what I hear
Far out? Now and then the foam there curls
And stretches a white arm out like a girl's.

Fishes and gulls ring no bells. There cannot be
A chapel or church between here and Devon,
With fishes or gulls ringing its bell,—hark.—
Somewhere under the sea or up in heaven.
"It's the bell, my son, out in the bay
On the buoy. It does sound sweet today."

Sweeter I never heard, mother, no, not in all Wales.
I should like to be lying under that foam,
Dead, but able to hear the sound of the bell,
And certain that you would often come
And rest, listening happily.
I should be happy if that could be.

The Bridge

I have come a long way today:
On a strange bridge alone,
Remembering friends, old friends,
I rest, without smile or moan,
As they remember me without smile or moan.

All are behind, the kind
And the unkind too, no more
Tonight than a dream. The stream
Runs softly yet drowns the Past,
The dark-lit stream has drowned the Future and the Past.

No traveller has rest more blest
Than this moment brief between
Two lives, when the Night's first lights
And shades hide what has never been,
Things goodlier, lovelier, dearer, than will be or have been.

Good-night

The skylarks are far behind that sang over the down;
I can hear no more those suburb nightingales;
Thrushes and blackbirds sing in the gardens of the town
In vain: the noise of man, beast, and machine prevails.

But the call of children in the unfamiliar streets
That echo with a familiar light echoing,
Sweet as the voice of nightingale or lark, completes
A magic of strange welcome, so that I seem a king

Among man, beast, machine, bird, child, and the ghost
That in the echo lives and with the echo dies.
The friendless town is friendly; homeless, I am not lost;
Though I know none of these doors, and meet but strangers'
    eyes.

Never again, perhaps, after tomorrow, shall
I see these homely streets, these church windows alight,
Not a man or woman or child among them all:
But it is All Friends' Night, a traveller's good night.

But These Things Also

But these things also are Spring's—
On banks by the roadside the grass
Long-dead that is greyer now
Than all the Winter it was;

The shell of a little snail bleached
In the grass; chip of flint, and mite
Of chalk; and the small birds' dung
In splashes of purest white:

All the white things a man mistakes
For earliest violets
Who seeks through Winter's ruins
Something to pay Winter's debts,

While the North blows, and starling flocks
By chattering on and on
Keep their spirits up in the mist,
And Spring's here, Winter's not gone.

The New House

Now first, as I shut the door,
I was alone
In the new house; and the wind
Began to moan.

Old at once was the house,
And I was old;
My ears were teased with the dread
Of what was foretold,

Nights of storm, days of mist, without end;
Sad days when the sun
Shone in vain: old griefs, and griefs
Not yet begun.

All was foretold me; naught
Could I foresee;
But I learnt how the wind would sound
After these things should be.

The Barn and the Down

It stood in the sunset sky
Like the straight-backed down,
Many a time—the barn
At the edge of the town,

So huge and dark that it seemed
It was the hill
Till the gable's precipice proved
It impossible.

Then the great down in the west
Grew into sight,
A barn stored full to the ridge
With black of night;

And the barn fell to a barn
Or even less
Before critical eyes and its own
Late mightiness.

But far down and near barn and I
Since then have smiled,
Having seen my new cautiousness
By itself beguiled

To disdain what seemed the barn
Till a few steps changed
It past all doubt to the down;
So the barn was avenged.

Sowing

It was a perfect day
For sowing; just
As sweet and dry was the ground
As tobacco-dust.

I tasted deep the hour
Between the far
Owl's chuckling first soft cry
And the first star.

A long stretched hour it was;
Nothing undone
Remained; the early seeds
All safely sown.

And now, hark at the rain,
Windless and light,
Half a kiss, half a tear,
Saying good-night.

March the Third

Here again (she said) is March the third
And twelve hours singing for the bird
'Twixt dawn and dusk, from half past six
To half past six, never unheard.

'Tis Sunday, and the church-bells end
With the birds' songs. I think they blend
Better than in the same fair days
That shall pronounce the Winter's end.

Do men mark, and none dares say,
How it may shift and long delay,
Somewhere before the first of Spring,
But never fails, this singing day?

When it falls on Sunday, bells
Are a wild natural voice that dwells
On hillsides; but the birds' songs have
The holiness gone from the bells.

This day unpromised is more dear
Than all the named days of the year
When seasonable sweets come in,
Since now we know how lucky we are.

Two Pewits

Under the after-sunset sky
Two pewits sport and cry,
More white than is the moon on high
Riding the dark surge silently;
More black than earth. Their cry
Is the one sound under the sky.
They alone move, now low, now high,
And merrily they cry
To the mischievous Spring sky,
Plunging earthward, tossing high,
Over the ghost who wonders why
So merrily they cry and fly,
Nor choose 'twixt earth and sky,
While the moon's quarter silently
Rides, and earth rests as silently.

Will You Come?

Will you come?
Will you come?
Will you ride
So late
At my side?
O, will you come?

Will you come?
Will you come
If the night
Has a moon,
Full and bright?
O, will you come?

Would you come?
Would you come
If the noon
Gave light,
Not the moon?
Beautiful, would you come?

Would you have come?
Would you have come
Without scorning,
Had it been
Still morning?
Beloved, would you have come?

If you come
Haste and come.
Owls have cried;
It grows dark
To ride,
Beloved, beautiful, come.

The Path

Running along a bank, a parapet
That saves from the precipitous wood below
The level road, there is a path. It serves
Children for looking down the long smooth steep,
Between the legs of beech and yew, to where
A fallen tree checks the sight: while men and women
Content themselves with the road and what they see
Over the bank, and what the children tell.
The path, winding like silver, trickles on,
Bordered and even invaded by thinnest moss
That tries to cover roots and crumbling chalk
With gold, olive, and emerald, but in vain.
The children wear it. They have flattened the bank
On top, and silvered it between the moss
With the current of their feet, year after year.
But the road is houseless, and leads not to school.
To see a child is rare there, and the eye
Has but the road, the wood that overhangs
And underyawns it, and the path that looks
As if it led on to some legendary
Or fancied place where men have wished to go
And stay; till, sudden, it ends where the wood ends.

The Wasp Trap

This moonlight makes
The lovely lovelier
Than ever before lakes
And meadows were.

And yet they are not,
Though this their hour is, more
Lovely than things that were not
Lovely before.

Nothing on earth,
And in the heavens no star,
For pure brightness is worth
More than that jar,

For wasps meant, now
A star—long may it swing
From the dead apple-bough,
So glistening.

A Tale [1]

There once the walls
Of the ruined cottage stood.
The periwinkle crawls
With flowers in its hair into the wood.

In flowerless hours
Never will the bank fail,
With everlasting flowers
On fragments of blue plates, to tell the tale.

[*published 1918; MS cancelled by Thomas*]

A Tale [2]

Here once flint walls,
Pump, orchard and wood pile stood.
Blue periwinkle crawls
From the last garden down into the wood.

The flowerless hours
Of Winter cannot prevail
To blight these other flowers,
Blue china fragments scattered, that tell the tale.

[*published 1978; revised version*]

Wind and Mist

They met inside the gateway that gives the view,
A hollow land as vast as heaven. "It is
A pleasant day, sir." "A very pleasant day."
"And what a view here. If you like angled fields
Of grass and grain bounded by oak and thorn,
Here is a league. Had we with Germany
To play upon this board it could not be
More dear than April has made it with a smile.
The fields beyond that league close in together
And merge, even as our days into the past,
Into one wood that has a shining pane
Of water. Then the hills of the horizon—
That is how I should make hills had I to show
One who would never see them what hills were like."
"Yes. Sixty miles of South Downs at one glance.
Sometimes a man feels proud at them, as if
He had just created them with one mighty thought."
"That house, though modern, could not be better planned
For its position. I never liked a new
House better. Could you tell me who lives in it?"
"No one." "Ah—and I was peopling all
Those windows on the south with happy eyes,
The terrace under them with happy feet;
Girls—" "Sir, I know. I know. I have seen that house
Through mist look lovely as a castle in Spain,
And airier. I have thought: ''Twere happy there
To live.' And I have laughed at that
Because I lived there then." "Extraordinary."
"Yes, with my furniture and family
Still in it, knowing every nook of it
And loving none, and in fact hating it."
"Dear me! How could that be? But pardon me."
"No offence. Doubtless the house was not to blame,

But the eye watching from those windows saw,
Many a day, day after day, mist—mist
Like chaos surging back—and felt itself
Alone in all the world, marooned alone.
We lived in clouds, on a cliff's edge almost
(You see), and if clouds went, the visible earth
Lay too far off beneath and like a cloud.
I did not know it was the earth I loved
Until I tried to live there in the clouds
And the earth turned to cloud."

                           "You had a garden
Of flint and clay, too." "True; that was real enough.
The flint was the one crop that never failed.
The clay first broke my heart, and then my back;
And the back heals not. There were other things
Real, too. In that room at the gable a child
Was born while the wind chilled a summer dawn:
Never looked grey mind on a greyer one
Than when the child's cry broke above the groans."
"I hope they were both spared." "They were. Oh yes.
But flint and clay and childbirth were too real
For this cloud castle. I had forgot the wind.
Pray do not let me get on to the wind.
You would not understand about the wind.
It is my subject, and compared with me
Those who have always lived on the firm ground
Are quite unreal in this matter of the wind.
There were whole days and nights when the wind and I
Between us shared the world, and the wind ruled
And I obeyed it and forgot the mist.
My past and the past of the world were in the wind.
Now you will say that though you understand
And feel for me, and so on, you yourself
Would find it different. You are all like that
If once you stand here free from wind and mist:

I might as well be talking to wind and mist.
You would believe the house-agent's young man
Who gives no heed to anything I say.
Good morning. But one word. I want to admit
That I would try the house once more, if I could;
As I should like to try being young again."

A Gentleman

"He has robbed two clubs. The judge at Salisbury
Can't give him more than he undoubtedly
Deserves. The scoundrel! Look at his photograph!
A lady-killer! Hanging's too good by half
For such as he." So said the stranger, one
With crimes yet undiscovered or undone.
But at the inn the Gypsy dame began:
"Now he was what I call a gentleman.
He went along with Carrie, and when she
Had a baby he paid up so readily
His half a crown. Just like him. A crown'd have been
More like him. For I never knew him mean.
Oh! but he was such a nice gentleman. Oh!
Last time we met he said if me and Joe
Was anywhere near we must be sure and call.
He put his arms around our Amos all
As if he were his own son. I pray God
Save him from justice! Nicer man never trod."

Lob

At hawthorn-time in Wiltshire travelling
In search of something chance would never bring,
An old man's face, by life and weather cut
And coloured,—rough, brown, sweet as any nut,—
A land face, sea-blue-eyed,—hung in my mind
When I had left him many a mile behind.
All he said was: "Nobody can't stop 'ee. It's
A footpath, right enough. You see those bits
Of mounds—that's where they opened up the barrows
Sixty years since, while I was scaring sparrows.
They thought as there was something to find there,
But couldn't find it, by digging, anywhere."

To turn back then and seek him, where was the use?
There were three Manningfords,—Abbots, Bohun, and Bruce:
And whether Alton, not Manningford, it was
My memory could not decide, because
There was both Alton Barnes and Alton Priors.
All had their churches, graveyards, farms, and byres,
Lurking to one side up the paths and lanes,
Seldom well seen except by aeroplanes;
And when bells rang, or pigs squealed, or cocks crowed,
Then only heard. Ages ago the road
Approached. The people stood and looked and turned,
Nor asked it to come nearer, nor yet learned
To move out there and dwell in all men's dust.
And yet withal they shot the weathercock, just
Because 'twas he crowed out of tune, they said:
So now the copper weathercock is dead.
If they had reaped their dandelions and sold
Them fairly, they could have afforded gold.

Many years passed, and I went back again

Among those villages, and I looked for men
Who might have known my ancient. He himself
Had long been dead or laid upon the shelf,
I thought. One man I asked about him roared
At my description: "'Tis old Bottlesford
He means, Bill." But another said: "Of course,
It was Jack Button up at the White Horse.
He's dead, sire, these three years." This last till
A girl proposed Walker of Walker's Hill,
"Old Adam Walker. Adam's Point you'll see
Marked on the maps."

                              "That was her roguery"
The next man said. He was a squire's son
Who loved wild bird and beast, and dog and gun
For killing them. He had loved them from his birth,
One with another, as he loved the earth.
"The man may be like Button, or Walker, or
Like Bottlesford, that you want, but far more
He sounds like one I saw when I was a child.
I could almost swear to him. The man was wild
And wandered. His home was where he was free.
Everybody has met one such man as he.
Does he keep clear old paths that no one uses
But once a life-time when he loves or muses?
He is English as this gate, these flowers, this mire.
And when at eight years old Lob-lie-by-the-fire
Came in my books, this was the man I saw.
He has been in England as long as dove and daw,
Calling the wild cherry tree the merry tree,
The rose campion Bridget-in-her-Bravery;
And in a tender mood he, as I guess,
Christened one flower Live-in-idleness,
And while he walked from Exeter to Leeds
One April called all cuckoo-flowers Milkmaids.

From him old herbal Gerard learnt, as a boy,
To name wild clematis the Traveller's-joy.
Our blackbirds sang no English till his ear
Told him they called his Jan Toy 'Pretty dear.'
(She was Jan Toy the Lucky, who, having lost
A shilling, and found a penny loaf, rejoiced.)
For reasons of his own to him the wren
Is Jenny Pooter. Before all other men
'Twas he first called the Hog's Back the Hog's Back.
That Mother Dunch's Buttocks should not lack
Their name was his care. He too could explain
Totteridge and Totterdown and Juggler's Lane:
He knows, if anyone. Why Tumbling Bay,
Inland in Kent, is called so, he might say.

"But little he says compared with what he does.
If ever a sage troubles him he will buzz
Like a beehive to conclude the tedious fray:
And the sage, who knows all languages, runs away.
Yet Lob has thirteen hundred names for a fool,
And though he never could spare time for school
To unteach what the fox so well expressed,
On biting the cock's head off,—Quietness is best,—
He can talk quite as well as anyone
After his thinking is forgot and done.
He first of all told someone else's wife,
For a farthing she'd skin a flint and spoil a knife
Worth sixpence skinning it. She heard him speak:
'She had a face as long as a wet week'
Said he, telling the tale in after years.
With blue smock and with gold rings in his ears,
Sometimes he is a pedlar, not too poor
To keep his wit. This is tall Tom that bore
The logs in, and with Shakespeare in the hall
Once talked, when icicles hung by the wall.

As Herne the Hunter he has known hard times.
On sleepless nights he made up weather rhymes
Which others spoilt. And, Hob, being then his name,
He kept the hog that thought the butcher came
To bring his breakfast. 'You thought wrong' said Hob.
When there were kings in Kent this very Lob,
Whose sheep grew fat and he himself grew merry,
Wedded the king's daughter of Canterbury;
For he alone, unlike squire, lord, and king,
Watched a night by her without slumbering;
He kept both waking. When he was but a lad
He won a rich man's heiress, deaf, dumb, and sad,
By rousing her to laugh at him. He carried
His donkey on his back. So they were married.
And while he was a little cobbler's boy
He tricked the giant coming to destroy
Shrewsbury by flood. 'And how far is it yet?'
The giant asked in passing. 'I forget;
But see these shoes I've worn out on the road
And we're not there yet.' He emptied out his load
Of shoes. The giant sighed, and dropped from his spade
The earth for damming Severn, and thus made
The Wrekin hill; and little Ercall hill
Rose where the giant scraped his boots. While still
So young, our Jack was chief of Gotham's sages.
But long before he could have been wise, ages
Earlier than this, while he grew thick and strong
And ate his bacon, or, at times, sang a song
And merely smelt it, as Jack the giant-killer
He made a name. He, too, ground up the miller,
The Yorkshireman who ground men's bones for flour.

"Do you believe Jack dead before his hour?
Or that his name is Walker, or Bottlesford,
Or Button, a mere clown, or squire, or lord?
The man you saw,—Lob-lie-by-the-fire, Jack Cade,
Jack Smith, Jack Moon, poor Jack of every trade,
Your Jack, or old Jack, or Jack What-d'ye-call,
Jack-in-the-hedge, or Robin-run-by-the-wall,
Robin Hood, Ragged Robin, lazy Bob,
One of the lords of No Man's Land, good Lob,—
Although he was seen dying at Waterloo,
Hastings, Agincourt, and Sedgemoor, too,—
Lives yet. He never will admit he is dead
Till millers cease to grind men's bones for bread,
Nor till our weathercock crows once again
And I remove my house out of the lane
On to the road." With this he disappeared
In hazel and thorn tangled with old-man's-beard.
But one glimpse of his back, as there he stood,
Choosing his way, proved him of old Jack's blood,
Young Jack perhaps, and now a Wiltshireman
As he has oft been since his days began.

Digging [1]

Today I think
Only with scents,—scents dead leaves yield,
And bracken, and wild carrot's seed,
And the square mustard field;

Odours that rise
When the spade wounds the roots of tree,
Rose, currant, raspberry, or goutweed,
Rhubarb or celery;

The smoke's smell, too,
Flowing from where a bonfire burns
The dead, the waste, the dangerous,
And all to sweetness turns.

It is enough
To smell, to crumble the dark earth,
While the robin sings over again
Sad songs of Autumn mirth.

Lovers

The two men in the road were taken aback.
The lovers came out shading their eyes from the sun,
And never was white so white, or black so black,
As her cheeks and hair. "There are more things than one
A man might turn into a wood for, Jack,"
Said George; Jack whispered: "He has not got a gun.
It's a bit too much of a good thing, I say.
They are going the other road, look. And see her run."—
She ran—"What a thing it is, this picking may."

In Memoriam (Easter 1915)

The flowers left thick at nightfall in the wood
This Eastertide call into mind the men,
Now far from home, who, with their sweethearts, should
Have gathered them and will do never again.

Head and Bottle

The downs will lose the sun, white alyssum
Lose the bees' hum;
But head and bottle tilted back in the cart
Will never part
Till I am cold as midnight and all my hours
Are beeless flowers.
He neither sees, nor hears, nor smells, nor thinks,
But only drinks,
Quiet in the yard where tree trunks do not lie
More quietly.

Home

Often I had gone this way before:
But now it seemed I never could be
And never had been anywhere else;
'Twas home; one nationality
We had, I and the birds that sang,
One memory.

They welcomed me. I had come back
That eve somehow from somewhere far:
The April mist, the chill, the calm,
Meant the same thing familiar
And pleasant to us, and strange too,
Yet with no bar.

The thrush on the oak top in the lane
Sang his last song, or last but one;
And as he ended, on the elm
Another had but just begun
His last; they knew no more than I
The day was done.

Then past his dark white cottage front
A labourer went along, his tread
Slow, half with weariness, half with ease;
And, through the silence, from his shed
The sound of sawing rounded all
That silence said.

Health

Four miles at a leap, over the dark hollow land,
To the frosted steep of the down and its junipers black,
Travels my eye with equal ease and delight:
And scarce could my body leap four yards.

This is the best and the worst of it—
Never to know,
Yet to imagine gloriously, pure health.

Today, had I suddenly health,
I could not satisfy the desire of my heart
Unless health abated it,
So beautiful is the air in its softness and clearness, while
    Spring
Promises all and fails in nothing as yet;
And what blue and what white is I never knew
Before I saw this sky blessing the land.

For had I health I could not ride or run or fly
So far or so rapidly over the land
As I desire: I should reach Wiltshire tired;
I should have changed my mind before I could be in Wales.
I could not love; I could not command love.
Beauty would still be far off
However many hills I climbed over;
Peace would be still farther.
Maybe I should not count it anything
To leap these four miles with the eye;
And either I should not be filled almost to bursting with
    desire,
Or with my power desire would still keep pace.

Yet I am not satisfied
Even with knowing I never could be satisfied.
With health and all the power that lies
In maiden beauty, poet and warrior,
In Caesar, Shakespeare, Alcibiades,
Mazeppa, Leonardo, Michelangelo,
In any maiden whose smile is lovelier
Than sunlight upon dew,
I could not be as the wagtail running up and down
The warm tiles of the roof slope, twittering
Happily and sweetly as if the sun itself
Extracted the song
As the hand makes sparks from the fur of a cat:

I could not be as the sun.
Nor should I be content to be
As little as the bird or as mighty as the sun.
For the bird knows not of the sun,
And the sun regards not the bird.
But I am almost proud to love both bird and sun,
Though scarce this Spring could my body leap four yards.

The Huxter

He has a hump like an ape on his back;
He has of money a plentiful lack;
And but for a gay coat of double his girth
There is not a plainer thing on the earth
    This fine May morning.

But the huxter has a bottle of beer;
He drives a cart and his wife sits near
Who does not heed his lack or his hump;
And they laugh as down the lane they bump
    This fine May morning.

She Dotes

She dotes on what the wild birds say
Or hint or mock at, night and day,—
Thrush, blackbird, all that sing in May,
    And songless plover,
Hawk, heron, owl, and woodpecker.
They never say a word to her
    About her lover.

She laughs at them for childishness,
She cries at them for carelessness
Who see her going loverless
    Yet sing and chatter
Just as when he was not a ghost,
Nor ever ask her what she has lost
    Or what is the matter.

Yet she has fancied blackbirds hide
A secret, and that thrushes chide
Because she thinks death can divide
    Her from her lover;
And she has slept, trying to translate
The word the cuckoo cries to his mate
    Over and over.

Song

She is beautiful
With happiness invincible:
If cruel she be
It is the hawk's proud innocent cruelty.

At poet's tears,
Sweeter than any smiles but hers,
She laughs; I sigh;
And yet I could not live if she should die.

And when in June
Once more the cuckoo spoils his tune,
She laughs at sighs;
And yet she says she loves me till she dies.

A Cat

She had a name among the children;
But no one loved though someone owned
Her, locked her out of doors at bedtime
And had her kittens duly drowned.

In Spring, nevertheless, this cat
Ate blackbirds, thrushes, nightingales,
And birds of bright voice and plume and flight,
As well as scraps from neighbours' pails.

I loathed and hated her for this;
One speckle on a thrush's breast
Was worth a million such; and yet
She lived long, till God gave her rest.

Melancholy

The rain and wind, the rain and wind, raved endlessly.
On me the Summer storm, and fever, and melancholy
Wrought magic, so that if I feared the solitude
Far more I feared all company: too sharp, too rude,
Had been the wisest or the dearest human voice.
What I desired I knew not, but whate'er my choice
Vain it must be, I knew. Yet naught did my despair
But sweeten the strange sweetness, while through the wild air
All day long I heard a distant cuckoo calling
And, soft as dulcimers, sounds of near water falling,
And, softer, and remote as if in history,
Rumours of what had touched my friends, my foes, or me.

Tonight

Harry, you know at night
The larks in Castle Alley
Sing from the attic's height
As if the electric light
Were the true sun above the summer valley:
Whistle, don't knock, tonight.

I shall come early, Kate;
And we in Castle Alley
Will sit close out of sight
Alone, and ask no light
Of lamp or sun above a summer valley:
Tonight I can stay late.

April

The sweetest thing, I thought
At one time, between earth and heaven
Was the first smile
When mist has been forgiven
And the sun has stolen out,
Peered, and resolved to shine at seven
On dabbled lengthening grasses,
Thick primroses and early leaves uneven,
When earth's breath, warm and humid, far surpasses
The richest oven's, and loudly rings "cuckoo"
And sharply the nightingale's "tsoo, troo, tsoo, troo":
To say "God bless it" was all that I could do.

But now I know one sweeter
By far since the day Emily
Turned weeping back
To me, still happy me,
To ask forgiveness,—
Yet smiled with half a certainty
To be forgiven,—for what
She had never done; I knew not what it might be,
Nor could she tell me, having now forgot,
By rapture carried with me past all care
As to an isle in April lovelier
Than April's self. "God bless you" I said to her.

The Glory

The glory of the beauty of the morning,—
The cuckoo crying over the untouched dew;
The blackbird that has found it, and the dove
That tempts me on to something sweeter than love;
White clouds ranged even and fair as new-mown hay;
The heat, the stir, the sublime vacancy
Of sky and meadow and forest and my own heart:—
The glory invites me, yet it leaves me scorning
All I can ever do, all I can be,
Beside the lovely of motion, shape, and hue,
The happiness I fancy fit to dwell
In beauty's presence. Shall I now this day
Begin to seek as far as heaven, as hell,
Wisdom or strength to match this beauty, start
And tread the pale dust pitted with small dark drops,
In hope to find whatever it is I seek,
Hearkening to short-lived happy-seeming things
That we know naught of, in the hazel copse?
Or must I be content with discontent
As larks and swallows are perhaps with wings?
And shall I ask at the day's end once more
What beauty is, and what I can have meant
By happiness? And shall I let all go,
Glad, weary, or both? Or shall I perhaps know
That I was happy oft and oft before,
Awhile forgetting how I am fast pent,
How dreary-swift, with naught to travel to,
Is Time? I cannot bite the day to the core.

July

Naught moves but clouds, and in the glassy lake
Their doubles and the shadow of my boat.
The boat itself stirs only when I break
This drowse of heat and solitude afloat
To prove if what I see be bird or mote,
Or learn if yet the shore woods be awake.

Long hours since dawn grew,—spread,—and passed on high
And deep below,—I have watched the cool reeds hung
Over images more cool in imaged sky:
Nothing there was worth thinking of so long;
All that the ring-doves say, far leaves among,
Brims my mind with content thus still to lie.

The Chalk Pit

"Is this the road that climbs above and bends
Round what was once a chalk pit: now it is
By accident an amphitheatre.
Some ash trees standing ankle-deep in brier
And bramble act the parts, and neither speak
Nor stir." "But see: they have fallen, every one,
And brier and bramble have grown over them."
"That is the place. As usual no one is here.
Hardly can I imagine the drop of the axe,
And the smack that is like an echo, sounding here."
"I do not understand." "Why, what I mean is
That I have seen the place two or three times
At most, and that its emptiness and silence
And stillness haunt me, as if just before
It was not empty, silent, still, but full
Of life of some kind, perhaps tragical.
Has anything unusual happened here?"
"Not that I know of. It is called the Dell.
They have not dug chalk here for a century.
That was the ash trees' age. But I will ask."
"No. Do not. I prefer to make a tale,
Or better leave it like the end of a play,
Actors and audience and lights all gone;
For so it looks now. In my memory
Again and again I see it, strangely dark,
And vacant of a life but just withdrawn.
We have not seen the woodman with the axe.
Some ghost has left it now as we two came."
"And yet you doubted if this were the road?"
"Well, sometimes I have thought of it and failed
To place it. No. And I am not quite sure,
Even now, this is it. For another place,
Real or painted, may have combined with it.

Or I myself a long way back in time . . ."
"Why, as to that, I used to meet a man—
I had forgotten,—searching for birds' nests
Along the road and in the chalk pit too.
The wren's hole was an eye that looked at him
For recognition. Every nest he knew.
He got a stiff neck, by looking this side or that,
Spring after spring, he told me, with his laugh,—
A sort of laugh. He was a visitor,
A man of forty,—smoked and strolled about.
At orts and crosses Pleasure and Pain had played
On his brown features;—I think both had lost;—
Mild and yet wild too. You may know the kind.
And once or twice a woman shared his walks,
A girl of twenty with a brown boy's face,
And hair brown as a thrush or as a nut,
Thick eyebrows, glinting eyes—" "You have said enough.
A pair,—free thought, free love,—I know the breed:
I shall not mix my fancies up with them."
"You please yourself. I should prefer the truth
Or nothing. Here, in fact, is nothing at all
Except a silent place that once rang loud,
And trees and us—imperfect friends, we men
And trees since time began; and nevertheless
Between us still we breed a mystery."

Fifty Faggots

There they stand, on their ends, the fifty faggots
That once were underwood of hazel and ash
In Jenny Pinks's Copse. Now, by the hedge
Close packed, they make a thicket fancy alone
Can creep through with the mouse and wren. Next Spring
A blackbird or a robin will nest there,
Accustomed to them, thinking they will remain
Whatever is for ever to a bird:
This Spring it is too late; the swift has come.
'Twas a hot day for carrying them up:
Better they will never warm me, though they must
Light several Winters' fires. Before they are done
The war will have ended, many other things
Have ended, maybe, that I can no more
Foresee or more control than robin and wren.

Sedge-Warblers [1]

This beauty made me dream there was a time
Long past and irrecoverable, a clime
Where any brook so radiant racing clear
Through buttercup and kingcup bright as brass
But gentle, nourishing the meadow grass
That leans and scurries in the wind, would bear
Another beauty, divine and feminine,
Child to the sun, a nymph whose soul unstained
Could love all day, and never hate or tire,
A lover of mortal or immortal kin.

And yet, rid of this dream, ere I had drained
Its poison, quieted was my desire
So that I only looked into the water,
Clearer than any goddess or man's daughter,
And hearkened while it combed the dark green hair
And shook the millions of the blossoms white
Of water-crowfoot, and curdled to one sheet
The flowers fallen from the chestnuts in the park
Far off. And sedge-warblers, clinging so light
To willow twigs, sang longer than the lark,
Quick, shrill, or grating, a song to match the heat
Of the strong sun, nor less the water's cool,
Gushing through narrows, swirling in the pool.
Their song that lacks all words, all melody,
All sweetness almost, was dearer then to me
Than sweetest voice that sings in tune sweet words.
This was the best of May—the small brown birds
Wisely reiterating endlessly
What no man learnt yet, in or out of school.

[*published 1918; MS canceled by Thomas*]

Sedge-Warblers [2]

This beauty makes me dream there was a time
Long past and irrecoverable, a clime
Where river of such radiance racing clear
Through buttercup and kingcup bright as brass
But gentle, nourishing the meadowgrass
That leans and scurries in the wind, would bear
Another beauty, divine and feminine,
Child of the sun, whose happy soul unstained
Could love all day, and never hate or tire,
Lover of mortal or immortal kin.

And yet rid of this dream, ere I had drained
Its poison, quieted was my desire
So that I only looked into the water
And hearkened, while it combed the dark-green hair
And shook the millions of the blossoms white
Of water crowfoot, and curdled in one sheet
The flowers fallen from the chestnuts in the park
Far off. The sedgewarblers that hung so light
On willow twigs, sang longer than any lark,
Quick, shrill or grating, a song to match the heat
Of the strong sun, nor less the water's cool
Gushing through narrows, swirling in the pool.
Their song that lacks all words, all melody,
All sweetness almost, was dearer now to me
Than sweetest voice that sings in tune sweet words:
This was the best of May, the small brown birds
Wisely reiterating endlessly
What no man learnt yet, in or out of school.

[*published 1978; revised version*]

I Built Myself a House of Glass

I built myself a house of glass:
It took me years to make it:
And I was proud. But now, alas,
Would God someone would break it.

But it looks too magnificent.
No neighbour casts a stone
From where he dwells, in tenement
Or palace of glass, alone.

Words

Out of us all
That make rhymes,
Will you choose
Sometimes—
As the winds use
A crack in the wall
Or a drain,
Their joy or their pain
To whistle through—
Choose me,
You English words?
I know you:
You are light as dreams,
Tough as oak,
Precious as gold,
As poppies and corn,
Or an old cloak:
Sweet as our birds
To the ear,
As the burnet rose
In the heat
Of Midsummer:
Strange as the races
Of dead and unborn:
Strange and sweet
Equally,
And familiar,
To the eye,
As the dearest faces
That a man knows,
And as lost homes are:
But though older far
Than oldest yew,—

As our hills are, old,—
Worn new
Again and again;
Young as our streams
After rain:
And as dear
As the earth which you prove
That we love.

Make me content
With some sweetness
From Wales
Whose nightingales
Have no wings,—
From Wiltshire and Kent
And Herefordshire,
And the villages there,—
From the names, and the things
No less.

Let me sometimes dance
With you,
Or climb
Or stand perchance
In ecstasy,
Fixed and free
In a rhyme,
As poets do.

The Word

There are so many things I have forgot,
That once were much to me, or that were not,
All lost, as is a childless woman's child
And its child's children, in the undefiled
Abyss of what can never be again.
I have forgot, too, names of the mighty men
That fought and lost or won in the old wars,
Of kings and fiends and gods, and most of the stars.
Some things I have forgot that I forget.
But lesser things there are, remembered yet,
Than all the others. One name that I have not—
Though 'tis an empty thingless name—forgot
Never can die because Spring after Spring
Some thrushes learn to say it as they sing.
There is always one at midday saying it clear
And tart—the name, only the name I hear.
While perhaps I am thinking of the elder scent
That is like food, or while I am content
With the wild rose scent that is like memory,
This name suddenly is cried out to me
From somewhere in the bushes by a bird
Over and over again, a pure thrush word.

Under the Woods

When these old woods were young
The thrushes' ancestors
As sweetly sung
In the old years.

There was no garden here,
Apples nor mistletoe;
No children dear
Ran to and fro.

New then was this thatched cot,
But the keeper was old,
And he had not
Much lead or gold.

Most silent beech and yew:
As he went round about
The woods to view
Seldom he shot.

But now that he is gone
Out of most memories,
Still lingers on
A stoat of his,

But one, shrivelled and green,
And with no scent at all,
And barely seen
On this shed wall.

Haymaking

After night's thunder far away had rolled
The fiery day had a kernel sweet of cold,
And in the perfect blue the clouds uncurled,
Like the first gods before they made the world
And misery, swimming the stormless sea
In beauty and in divine gaiety.
The smooth white empty road was lightly strewn
With leaves—the holly's Autumn falls in June—
And fir cones standing stiff up in the heat.
The mill-foot water tumbled white and lit
With tossing crystals, happier than any crowd
Of children pouring out of school aloud.
And in the little thickets where a sleeper
For ever might lie lost, the nettle-creeper
And garden warbler sang unceasingly;
While over them shrill shrieked in his fierce glee
The swift with wings and tail as sharp and narrow
As if the bow had flown off with the arrow.
Only the scent of woodbine and hay new-mown
Travelled the road. In the field sloping down,
Park-like, to where its willows showed the brook,
Haymakers rested. The tosser lay forsook
Out in the sun; and the long waggon stood
Without its team; it seemed it never would
Move from the shadow of that single yew.
The team, as still, until their task was due,
Beside the labourers enjoyed the shade
That three squat oaks mid-field together made
Upon a circle of grass and weed uncut,
And on the hollow, once a chalk-pit, but
Now brimmed with nut and elder-flower so clean.
The men leaned on their rakes, about to begin,
But still. And all were silent. All was old,

This morning time, with a great age untold,
Older than Clare and Cowper, Morland and Crome,
Than, at the field's far edge, the farmer's home,
A white house crouched at the foot of a great tree.
Under the heavens that know not what years be
The men, the beasts, the trees, the implements
Uttered even what they will in times far hence—
All of us gone out of the reach of change—
Immortal in a picture of an old grange.

A Dream

Over known fields with an old friend in dream
I walked, but came sudden to a strange stream.
Its dark waters were bursting out most bright
From a great mountain's heart into the light.
They ran a short course under the sun, then back
Into a pit they plunged, once more as black
As at their birth: and I stood thinking there
How white, had the day shone on them, they were,
Heaving and coiling. So by the roar and hiss
And by the mighty motion of the abyss
I was bemused, that I forgot my friend
And neither saw nor sought him till the end,
When I awoke from waters unto men
Saying: "I shall be here some day again."

The Brook

Seated once by a brook, watching a child
Chiefly that paddled, I was thus beguiled.
Mellow the blackbird sang and sharp the thrush
Not far off in the oak and hazel brush,
Unseen. There was a scent like honeycomb
From mugwort dull. And down upon the dome
Of the stone the cart-horse kicks against so oft
A butterfly alighted. From aloft
He took the heat of the sun, and from below.
On the hot stone he perched contented so,
As if never a cart would pass again
That way; as if I were the last of men
And he the first of insects to have earth
And sun together and to know their worth.
I was divided between him and the gleam,
The motion, and the voices, of the stream,
The waters running frizzled over gravel,
That never vanish and for ever travel.
A grey flycatcher silent on a fence
And I sat as if we had been there since
The horseman and the horse lying beneath
The fir-tree-covered barrow on the heath,
The horseman and the horse with silver shoes,
Galloped the downs last. All that I could lose
I lost. And then the child's voice raised the dead.
"No one's been here before" was what she said
And what I felt, yet never should have found
A word for, while I gathered sight and sound.

Aspens

All day and night, save winter, every weather,
Above the inn, the smithy, and the shop,
The aspens at the cross-roads talk together
Of rain, until their last leaves fall from the top.

Out of the blacksmith's cavern comes the ringing
Of hammer, shoe, and anvil; out of the inn
The clink, the hum, the roar, the random singing—
The sounds that for these fifty years have been.

The whisper of the aspens is not drowned,
And over lightless pane and footless road,
Empty as sky, with every other sound
Not ceasing, calls their ghosts from their abode,

A silent smithy, a silent inn, nor fails
In the bare moonlight or the thick-furred gloom,
In tempest or the night of nightingales,
To turn the cross-roads to a ghostly room.

And it would be the same were no house near.
Over all sorts of weather, men, and times,
Aspens must shake their leaves and men may hear
But need not listen, more than to my rhymes.

Whatever wind blows, while they and I have leaves
We cannot other than an aspen be
That ceaselessly, unreasonably grieves,
Or so men think who like a different tree.

The Mill-Water

Only the sound remains
Of the old mill;
Gone is the wheel;
On the prone roof and walls the nettle reigns.

Water that toils no more
Dangles white locks
And, falling, mocks
The music of the mill-wheel's busy roar.

Pretty to see, by day
Its sound is naught
Compared with thought
And talk and noise of labour and of play.

Night makes the difference.
In calm moonlight,
Gloom infinite,
The sound comes surging in upon the sense:

Solitude, company,—
When it is night,—
Grief or delight
By it must haunted or concluded be.

Often the silentness
Has but this one
Companion;
Wherever one creeps in the other is:

Sometimes a thought is drowned
By it, sometimes
Out of it climbs;
All thoughts begin or end upon this sound,

Only the idle foam
Of water falling
Changelessly calling,
Where once men had a work-place and a home.

For These

An acre of land between the shore and the hills,
Upon a ledge that shows my kingdoms three,
The lovely visible earth and sky and sea,
Where what the curlew needs not, the farmer tills:

A house that shall love me as I love it,
Well-hedged, and honoured by a few ash-trees
That linnets, greenfinches, and goldfinches
Shall often visit and make love in and flit:

A garden I need never go beyond,
Broken but neat, whose sunflowers every one
Are fit to be the sign of the Rising Sun:
A spring, a brook's bend, or at least a pond:

For these I ask not, but, neither too late
Nor yet too early, for what men call content,
And also that something may be sent
To be contented with, I ask of fate.

Digging [2]

What matter makes my spade for tears or mirth,
Letting down two clay pipes into the earth?
The one I smoked, the other a soldier
Of Blenheim, Ramillies, and Malplaquet
Perhaps. The dead man's immortality
Lies represented lightly with my own,
A yard or two nearer the living air
Than bones of ancients who, amazed to see
Almighty God erect the mastodon,
Once laughed, or wept, in this same light of day.

Two Houses

Between a sunny bank and the sun
The farmhouse smiles
On the riverside plat:
No other one
So pleasant to look at
And remember, for many miles,
So velvet-hushed and cool under warm tiles.

Nor far from the road it lies, yet caught
Far out of reach
Of the road's dust
And the dusty thought
Of passers-by, though each
Stops, and turns, and must
Look down at it like a wasp at a muslined peach.

But another house stood there long before:
And as if above graves
Still the turf heaves
Above its stones:
Dark hangs the sycamore,
Shadowing kennel and bones
And the black dog that shakes his chain and moans.

And when he barks, over the river
Flashing fast,
Dark echoes reply,
And the hollow past
Half yields the dead that never
More than half hidden lie:
And out they creep and back again for ever.

Cock-Crow

Out of the wood of thoughts that grows by night
To be cut down by the sharp axe of light,—
Out of the night, two cocks together crow,
Cleaving the darkness with a silver blow:
And bright before my eyes twin trumpeters stand,
Heralds of splendour, one at either hand,
Each facing each as in a coat of arms:
The milkers lace their boots up at the farms.

October

The green elm with the one great bough of gold
Lets leaves into the grass slip, one by one.—
The short hill grass, the mushrooms small milk-white,
Harebell and scabious and tormentil,
That blackberry and gorse, in dew and sun,
Bow down to; and the wind travels too light
To shake the fallen birch leaves from the fern;
The gossamers wander at their own will.
At heavier steps than birds' the squirrels scold.

The late year has grown fresh again and new
As Spring, and to the touch is not more cool
Than it is warm to the gaze; and now I might
As happy be as earth is beautiful,
Were I some other or with earth could turn
In alternation of violet and rose,
Harebell and snowdrop, at their season due,
And gorse that has no time not to be gay.
But if this be not happiness, who knows?
Some day I shall think this a happy day,
And this mood by the name of melancholy
Shall no more blackened and obscured be.

There's Nothing Like the Sun

There's nothing like the sun as the year dies,
Kind as it can be, this world being made so,
To stones and men and beasts and birds and flies,
To all things that it touches except snow,
Whether on mountain side or street of town.
The south wall warms me: November has begun,
Yet never shone the sun as fair as now
While the sweet last-left damsons from the bough
With spangles of the morning's storm drop down
Because the starling shakes it, whistling what
Once swallows sang. But I have not forgot
That there is nothing, too, like March's sun,
Like April's, or July's, or June's, or May's,
Or January's, or February's, great days:
And August, September, October, and December
Have equal days, all different from November.
No day of any month but I have said—
Or, if I could live long enough, should say—
"There's nothing like the sun that shines today."
There's nothing like the sun till we are dead.

The Thrush

When Winter's ahead,
What can you read in November
That you read in April
When Winter's dead?

I hear the thrush, and I see
Him alone at the end of the lane
Near the bare poplar's tip,
Singing continuously.

Is it more that you know
Than that, even as in April,
So in November,
Winter is gone that must go?

Or is all your lore
Not to call November November,
And April April,
And Winter Winter—no more?

But I know the months all,
And their sweet names, April,
May and June and October,
As you call and call

I must remember
What died into April
And consider what will be born
Of a fair November;

And April I love for what
It was born of, and November
For what it will die in,
What they are and what they are not,

While you love what is kind,
What you can sing in
And love and forget in
All that's ahead and behind.

Liberty

The last light has gone out of the world, except
This moonlight lying on the grass like frost
Beyond the brink of the tall elm's shadow.
It is as if everything else had slept
Many an age, unforgotten and lost
The men that were, the things done, long ago,
All I have thought; and but the moon and I
Live yet and here stand idle over the grave
Where all is buried. Both have liberty
To dream what we could do if we were free
To do some thing we had desired long,
The moon and I. There's none less free than who
Does nothing and has nothing else to do,
Being free only for what is not to his mind,
And nothing is to his mind. If every hour
Like this one passing that I have spent among
The wiser others when I have forgot
To wonder whether I was free or not,
Were piled before me, and not lost behind,
And I could take and carry them away
I should be rich; or if I had the power
To wipe out every one and not again
Regret, I should be rich to be so poor.
And yet I still am half in love with pain,
With what is imperfect, with both tears and mirth,
With things that have an end, with life and earth,
And this moon that leaves me dark within the door.

This Is No Case of Petty Right or Wrong

This is no case of petty right or wrong
That politicians or philosophers
Can judge. I hate not Germans, nor grow hot
With love of Englishmen, to please newspapers.
Beside my hate for one fat patriot
My hatred of the Kaiser is love true:—
A kind of god he is, banging a gong.
But I have not to choose between the two,
Or between justice and injustice. Dinned
With war and argument I read no more
Than in the storm smoking along the wind
Athwart the wood. Two witches' cauldrons roar.
From one the weather shall rise clear and gay;
Out of the other an England beautiful
And like her mother that died yesterday.
Little I know or care if, being dull,
I shall miss something that historians
Can rake out of the ashes when perchance
The phoenix broods serene above their ken.
But with the best and meanest Englishmen
I am one in crying, God save England, lest
We lose what never slaves and cattle blessed.
The ages made her that made us from the dust:
She is all we know and live by, and we trust
She is good and must endure, loving her so:
And as we love ourselves we hate her foe.

Rain

Rain, midnight rain, nothing but the wild rain
On this bleak hut, and solitude, and me
Remembering again that I shall die
And neither hear the rain nor give it thanks
For washing me cleaner than I have been
Since I was born into this solitude.
Blessed are the dead that the rain rains upon:
But here I pray that none whom once I loved
Is dying tonight or lying still awake
Solitary, listening to the rain,
Either in pain or thus in sympathy
Helpless among the living and the dead,
Like a cold water among broken reeds,
Myriads of broken reeds all still and stiff,
Like me who have no love which this wild rain
Has not dissolved except the love of death,
If love it be towards what is perfect and
Cannot, the tempest tells me, disappoint.

Song

The clouds that are so light,
Beautiful, swift and bright,
Cast shadows on field and park
Of the earth that is so dark,

And even so now, light one!
Beautiful, swift and bright one!
You let fall on a heart that was dark,
Unillumined, a deeper mark.

But clouds would have, without earth
To shadow, far less worth:
Away from your shadow on me
Your beauty less would be,

And if it still be treasured
An age hence, it shall be measured
By this small dark spot
Without which it were not.

Roads

I love roads:
The goddesses that dwell
Far along invisible
Are my favorite gods.

Roads go on
While we forget, and are
Forgotten like a star
That shoots and is gone.

On this earth 'tis sure
We men have not made
Anything that doth fade
So soon, so long endure:

The hill road wet with rain
In the sun would not gleam
Like a winding stream
If we trod it not again.

They are lonely
While we sleep, lonelier
For lack of a traveller
Who is now a dream only.

From dawn's twilight
And all the clouds like sheep
On the mountains of sleep
They wind into the night.

The next turn may reveal
Heaven: upon the crest
The close pine clump, at rest
And black, may Hell conceal.

Often footsore, never
Yet of the road I weary,
Though long and steep and dreary
As it winds on for ever.

Helen of the roads,
The mountain ways of Wales
And the Mabinogion tales
Is one of the true gods,

Abiding in the trees,
The threes and fours so wise,
The larger companies,
That by the roadside be,

And beneath the rafter
Else uninhabited
Excepting by the dead;
And it is her laughter

At morn and night I hear
When the thrush cock sings
Bright irrelevant things,
And when the chanticleer

Calls back to their own night
Troops that make loneliness
With their light footsteps' press,
As Helen's own are light.

Now all roads lead to France
And heavy is the tread
Of the living; but the dead
Returning lightly dance:

Whatever the road bring
To me or take from me,
They keep me company
With their pattering,

Crowding the solitude
Of the loops over the downs,
Hushing the roar of towns
And their brief multitude.

The Ash Grove

Half of the grove stood dead, and those that yet lived made
Little more than the dead ones made of shade.
If they led to a home, long before they had seen its fall:
But they welcomed me; I was glad without cause and delayed.

Scarce a hundred paces under the trees was the interval—
Paces each sweeter than sweetest miles—but nothing at all,
Not even the spirits of memory and fear with restless wing,
Could climb down in to molest me over the wall

That I passed through at either end without noticing.
And now an ash grove far from those hills can bring
The same tranquillity in which I wander a ghost
With a ghostly gladness, as if I heard a girl sing

The song of the Ash Grove soft as love uncrossed,
And then in a crowd or in distance it were lost,
But the moment unveiled something unwilling to die
And I had what most I desired, without search or desert or cost.

February Afternoon

Men heard this roar of parleying starlings, saw,
A thousand years ago even as now,
Black rooks with white gulls following the plough
So that the first are last until a caw
Commands that last are first again,—a law
Which was of old when one, like me, dreamed how
A thousand years might dust lie on his brow
Yet thus would birds do between hedge and shaw.

Time swims before me, making as a day
A thousand years, while the broad ploughland oak
Roars mill-like and men strike and bear the stroke
Of war as ever, audacious or resigned,
And God still sits aloft in the array
That we have wrought him, stone-deaf and stone-blind.

P. H. T.

I may come near loving you
When you are dead
And there is nothing to do
And much to be said.

To repent that day will be
Impossible
For you, and vain for me
The truth to tell.

I shall be sorry for
Your impotence:
You can do and undo no more
When you go hence,

Cannot even forgive
The funeral.
But not so long as you live
Can I love you at all.

These Things that Poets Said

These things that poets said
Of love seemed true to me
When I loved and I fed
On love and poetry equally.

But now I wish I knew
If theirs were love indeed,
Of if mine were the true
And theirs some other lovely weed:

For certainly not thus,
Then or thereafter, I
Loved ever. Between us
Decide, good Love, before I die.

Only, that once I loved
By this one argument
Is very plainly proved:
I, loving not, am different.

No One So Much As You

No one so much as you
Love this my clay,
Or would lament as you
Its dying day.

You know me through and through
Though I have not told,
And though with what you know
You are not bold.

None ever was so fair
As I thought you:
Not a word can I bear
Spoken against you.

All that I ever did
For you seemed coarse
Compared with what I hid
Nor put in force.

Scarce my eyes dare meet you
Lest they should prove
I but respond to you
And do not love.

We look and understand,
We cannot speak
Except in trifles and
Words the most weak.

I at the most accept
Your love, regretting
That is all: I have kept
A helpless fretting

That I could not return
All that you gave
And could not ever burn
With the love you have,

Till sometimes it did seem
Better it were
Never to see you more
Than linger here

With only gratitude
Instead of love—
A pine in solitude
Cradling a dove.

The Unknown

She is most fair,
And when they see her pass
The poets' ladies
Look no more in the glass
But after her.

On a bleak moor
Running under the moon
She lures a poet,
Once proud or happy, soon
Far from his door.

Beside a train,
Because they saw her go,
Or failed to see her,
Travellers and watchers know
Another pain.

The simple lack
Of her is more to me
Than others' presence
Whether life splendid be
Or utter black.

I have not seen,
I have no news of her;
I can tell only
She is not here, but there
She might have been.

She is to be kissed
Only perhaps by me;
She may be seeking
Me and no other; she
May not exist.

Celandine

Thinking of her had saddened me at first,
Until I saw the sun on the celandines lie
Redoubled, and she stood up like a flame,
A living thing, not what before I nursed,
The shadow I was growing to love almost,
The phantom, not the creature with bright eye
That I had thought never to see, once lost.

She found the celandines of February
Always before us all. Her nature and name
Were like those flowers, and now immediately
For a short swift eternity back she came,
Beautiful, happy, simply as when she wore
Her brightest bloom among the winter hues
Of all the world; and I was happy too,
Seeing the blossoms and the maiden who
Had seen them with me Februarys before,
Bending to them as in and out she trod
And laughed, with locks sweeping the mossy sod.

But this was a dream: the flowers were not true,
Until I stooped to pluck from the grass there
One of five petals and I smelt the juice
Which made me sigh, remembering she was no more,
Gone like a never perfectly recalled air.

"Home"

Fair was the morning, fair our tempers, and
We had seen nothing fairer than the land,
Though strange, and the untrodden snow that made
Wild of the tame, casting out all that was
Not wild and rustic and old; and we were glad.

Fair too was afternoon, and first to pass
Were we that league of snow, next the north wind.

There was nothing to return for except need.
And yet we sang nor ever stopped for speed,
As we did often with the start behind.
Faster still strode we when we came in sight
Of the cold roofs where we must spend the night.

Happy we had not been there, nor could be,
Though we had tasted sleep and food and fellowship
Together long.
             "How quick" to someone's lip
The word came, "will the beaten horse run home."

The word "home" raised a smile in us all three,
And one repeated it, smiling just so
That all knew what he meant and none would say.
Between three counties far apart that lay
We were divided and looked strangely each
At the other, and we knew we were not friends
But fellows in a union that ends
With the necessity for it, as it ought.

Never a word was spoken, not a thought
Was thought, of what the look meant with the word
"Home" as we walked and watched the sunset blurred.
And then to me the word, only the word,
"Homesick," as it were playfully occurred:
No more. If I should ever more admit
Than the mere word I could not endure it
For a day longer: this captivity
Must somehow come to an end, else I should be
Another man, as often now I seem,
Or this life be only an evil dream.

Thaw

Over the land freckled with snow half-thawed
The speculating rooks at their nests cawed
And saw from elm-tops, delicate as flower of grass,
What we below could not see, Winter pass.

Household Poems

Bronwen

If I should ever by chance grow rich
I'll buy Codham, Cockridden, and Childerditch,
Roses, Pyrgo, and Lapwater,
And let them all to my elder daughter.
The rent I shall ask of her will be only
Each year's first violets, white and lonely,
The first primroses and orchises—
She must find them before I do, that is.
But if she finds a blossom on furze
Without rent they shall all for ever be hers,
Codham, Cockridden, and Childerditch,
Roses, Pyrgo and Lapwater,—
I shall give them all to my elder daughter.

Merfyn

If I were to own this countryside
As far as a man in a day could ride,
And the Tyes were mine for giving or letting,—
Wingle Tye and Margaretting
Tye,—and Skreens, Gooshays, and Cockerells,
Shellow, Rochetts, Bandish, and Pickerells,
Martins, Lambkins, and Lillyputs,
Their copses, ponds, roads, and ruts,
Fields where plough-horses steam and plovers
Fling and whimper, hedges that lovers
Love, and orchards, shrubberies, walls
Where the sun untroubled by north wind falls,
And single trees where the thrush sings well
His proverbs untranslatable,
I would give them all to my son
If he would let me any one
For a song, a blackbird's song, at dawn.
He should have no more, till on my lawn
Never a one was left, because I
Had shot them to put them into a pie,—
His Essex blackbirds, every one,
And I was left old and alone.

Then unless I could pay, for rent, a song
As sweet as a blackbird's, and as long—
No more—he should have the house, not I:
Margaretting or Wingle Tye,
Or it might be Skreens, Gooshays, or Cockerells,
Shellow, Rochetts, Bandish, or Pickerells,
Martins, Lambkins, or Lillyputs,
Should be his till the cart tracks had no ruts.

Myfanwy

What shall I give my daughter the younger
More than will keep her from cold and hunger?
I shall not give her anything.
If she shared South Weald and Havering,
Their acres, the two brooks running between,
Paine's Brook and Weald Brook,
With pewit, woodpecker, swan, and rook,
She would be no richer than the queen
Who once on a time sat in Havering Bower
Alone, with the shadows, pleasure and power.
She could do no more with Samarcand,
Or the mountains of a mountain land
And its far white house above cottages
Like Venus above the Pleiades.
Her small hands I would not cumber
With so many acres and their lumber,
But leave her Steep and her own world
And her spectacled self with hair uncurled,
Wanting a thousand little things
That time without contentment brings.

Helen

And you, Helen, what should I give you?
So many things I would give you
Had I an infinite great store
Offered me and I stood before
To choose. I would give you youth,
All kinds of loveliness and truth,
A clear eye as good as mine,
Lands, waters, flowers, wine,
As many children as your heart
Might wish for, a far better art
Than mine can be, all you have lost
Upon the travelling waters tossed,
Or given to me. If I could choose
Freely in that great treasure-house
Anything from any shelf,
I would give you back yourself,
And power to discriminate
What you want and want it not too late,
Many fair days free from care
And heart to enjoy both foul and fair,
And myself, too, if I could find
Where it lay hidden and it proved kind.

The Wind's Song

Dull-thoughted, walking among the nunneries
Of many a myriad anemones
In the close copses, I grew weary of Spring
Till I emerged and in my wandering
I climbed the down up to a lone pine clump
Of six, the tallest dead, one a mere stump.
On one long stem, branchless and flayed and prone
I sat in the sun listening to the wind alone,
Thinking there could be no old song so sad
As the wind's song; but later none so glad
Could I remember as that same wind's song
All the time blowing the pine boughs among.
My heart that had been still as the dead tree
Awakened by the West wind was made free.

Like the Touch of Rain

Like the touch of rain she was
On a man's flesh and hair and eyes
When the joy of walking thus
Has taken him by surprise:

With the love of the storm he burns,
He sings, he laughs, well I know how,
But forgets when he returns
As I shall not forget her "Go now."

Those two words shut a door
Between me and the blessed rain
That was never shut before
And will not open again.

When We Two Walked

When we two walked in Lent
We imagined that happiness
Was something different
And this was something less.

But happy were we to hide
Our happiness, not as they were
Who acted in their pride
Juno and Jupiter:

For the gods in their jealousy
Murdered that wife and man,
And we that were wise live free
To recall our happiness then.

Tall Nettles

Tall nettles cover up, as they have done
These many springs, the rusty harrow, the plough
Long worn out, and the roller made of stone:
Only the elm butt tops the nettles now.

This corner of the farmyard I like most:
As well as any bloom upon a flower
I like the dust on the nettles, never lost
Except to prove the sweetness of a shower.

The Watchers

By the ford at the town's edge
Horse and carter rest:
The carter smokes on the bridge
Watching the water press in swathes about his horse's chest.

From the inn one watches, too,
In the room for visitors
That has no fire, but a view
And many cases of stuffed fish, vermin, and kingfishers.

I Never Saw that Land Before

I never saw that land before,
And now can never see it again;
Yet, as if by acquaintance hoar
Endeared, by gladness and by pain,
Great was the affection that I bore

To the valley and the river small,
The cattle, the grass, the bare ash trees,
The chickens from the farmsteads, all
Elm-hidden, and the tributaries
Descending at equal interval;

The blackthorns down along the brook
With wounds yellow as crocuses
Where yesterday the labourer's hook
Had sliced them cleanly; and the breeze
That hinted all and nothing spoke.

I neither expected anything
Nor yet remembered: but some goal
I touch then; and if I could sing
What would not even whisper my soul
As I went on my journeying,

I should use, as the trees and birds did,
A language not to be betrayed;
And what was hid should still be hid
Excepting from those like me made
Who answer when such whispers bid.

The Cherry Trees

The cherry trees bend over and are shedding
On the old road where all that passed are dead,
Their petals, strewing the grass as for a wedding
This early May morn when there is none to wed.

It Rains

It rains, and nothing stirs within the fence
Anywhere through the orchard's untrodden, dense
Forest of parsley. The great diamonds
Of rain on the grassblades there is none to break,
Or the fallen petals further down to shake.

And I am nearly as happy as possible
To search the wilderness in vain though well,
To think of two walking, kissing there,
Drenched, yet forgetting the kisses of the rain:
Sad, too, to think that never, never again,

Unless alone, so happy shall I walk
In the rain. When I turn away, on its fine stalk
Twilight has fined to naught, the parsley flower
Figures, suspended still and ghostly white,
The past hovering as it revisits the light.

Some Eyes Condemn

Some eyes condemn the earth they gaze upon:
Some wait patiently till they know far more
Than earth can tell them: some laugh at the whole
As folly of another's making: one
I knew that laughed because he saw, from core
To rind, not one thing worth the laugh his soul
Had ready at waking: some eyes have begun
With laughing; some stand started at the door.

Others, too, I have seen rest, question, roll,
Dance, shoot. And many I have loved watching. Some
I could not take my eyes from till they turned
And loving died. I had not found my goal.
But thinking of your eyes, dear, I become
Dumb: for they flamed, and it was me they burned.

The Sun Used To Shine

The sun used to shine while we two walked
Slowly together, paused and started
Again, and sometimes mused, sometimes talked
As either pleased, and cheerfully parted

Each night. We never disagreed
Which gate to rest on. The to be
And the late past we gave small heed.
We turned from men or poetry

To rumours of the war remote
Only till both stood disinclined
For aught but the yellow flavorous coat
Of an apple wasps had undermined;

Or a sentry of dark betonies,
The stateliest of small flowers on earth,
At the forest verge; or crocuses
Pale purple as if they had their birth

In sunless Hades fields. The war
Came back to mind with the moonrise
Which soldiers in the east afar
Beheld then. Nevertheless, our eyes

Could as well imagine the Crusades
Or Caesar's battles. Everything
To faintness like those rumours fades—
Like the brook's water glittering

Under the moonlight—like those walks
Now—like us two that took them, and
The fallen apples, all the talks
And silences—like memory's sand

When the tide covers it late or soon,
And other men through other flowers
In those fields under the same moon
Go talking and have easy hours.

No One Cares Less Than I

"No one cares less than I,
Nobody knows but God
Whether I am destined to lie
Under a foreign clod"
Were the words I made to the bugle call in the morning.

But laughing, storming, scorning,
Only the bugles know
What the bugles say in the morning,
And they do not care, when they blow
The call that I heard and made words to early this morning.

As the Team's Head-Brass

As the team's head-brass flashed out on the turn
The lovers disappeared into the wood.
I sat among the boughs of the fallen elm
That strewed an angle of the fallow, and
Watched the plough narrowing a yellow square
Of charlock. Every time the horses turned
Instead of treading me down, the ploughman leaned
Upon the handles to say or ask a word,
About the weather, next about the war.
Scraping the share he faced towards the wood,
And screwed along the furrow till the brass flashed
Once more.
    The blizzard felled the elm whose crest
I sat in, by a woodpecker's round hole,
The ploughman said. "When will they take it away?"
"When the war's over." So the talk began—
One minute and an interval of ten,
A minute more and the same interval.
"Have you been out?" "No." "And don't want to, perhaps?"
"If I could only come back again, I should.
I could spare an arm. I shouldn't want to lose
A leg. If I should lose my head, why, so,
I should want nothing more. . . . Have many gone
From here?" "Yes." "Many lost?" "Yes, a good few.
Only two teams work on the farm this year.
One of my mates is dead. The second day
In France they killed him. It was back in March,
The very night of the blizzard, too. Now if
He had stayed here we should have moved the tree."
"And I should not have sat here. Everything
Would have been different. For it would have been
Another world." "Ay, and a better, though
If we could see all all might seem good." Then

The lovers came out of the wood again:
The horses started and for the last time
I watched the clods crumble and topple over
After the ploughshare and the stumbling team.

After You Speak

After you speak
And what you meant
Is plain,
My eyes
Meet yours that mean—
With your cheeks and hair—
Something more wise,
More dark,
And far different.
Even so the lark
Loves dust
And nestles in it
The minute
Before he must
Soar in lone flight
So far,
Like a black star
He seems—
A mote
Of singing dust
Afloat
Above,
That dreams
And sheds no light.
I know your lust
Is love.

The Pond

Bright clouds of may
Shade half the pond.
Beyond,
All but one bay
Of emerald
Tall reeds
Like criss-cross bayonets
Where a bird once called,
Lies bright as the sun.
No one heeds.
The light wind frets
And drifts the scum
Of may-blossom.
Till the moorhen calls
Again
Naught's to be done
By birds or men.
Still the may falls.

Song

Early one morning in May I set out,
And nobody I knew was about.
    I'm bound away for ever,
      Away somewhere, away for ever.

There was no wind to trouble the weathercocks.
I had burnt my letters and darned my socks.

No one knew I was going away,
I thought myself I should come back some day.

I heard the brook through the town gardens run.
O sweet was the mud turned to dust by the sun.

A gate banged in a fence and banged in my head.
"A fine morning, sir," a shepherd said.

I could not return from my liberty,
To my youth and my love and my misery.

The past is the only dead thing that smells sweet,
The only sweet thing that is not also fleet.
    I'm bound away for ever,
      Away somewhere, away for ever.

It Was Upon

It was upon a July evening.
At a stile I stood, looking along a path
Over the country by a second Spring
Drenched perfect green again. "The lattermath
Will be a fine one." So the stranger said,
A wandering man. Albeit I stood at rest
Flushed with desire I was. The earth outspread,
Like meadows of the future, I possessed.

And as an unaccomplished prophecy
The stranger's words, after the interval
Of a score years, when those fields are by me
Never to be recrossed, now I recall,
This July eve, and question, wondering,
What of the lattermath to this hoar Spring?

Women He Liked

Women he liked, did shovel-bearded Bob,
Old Farmer Hayward of the Heath, but he
Loved horses. He himself was like a cob,
And leather-coloured. Also he loved a tree.

For the life in them he loved most living things,
But a tree chiefly. All along the lane
He planted elms where now the stormcock sings
That travellers hear from the slow-climbing train.

Till then the track had never had a name
For all its thicket and the nightingales
That should have earned it. No one was to blame.
To name a thing beloved man sometimes fails.

Many years since, Bob Hayward died, and now
None passes there because the mist and the rain
Out of the elms have turned the lane to slough
And gloom, the name alone survives, Bob's Lane.

There Was a Time

There was a time when this poor frame was whole
And I had youth and never another care,
Or none that should have troubled a strong soul.
Yet, except sometimes in a frosty air
When my heels hammered out a melody
From pavements of a city left behind,
I never would acknowledge my own glee
Because it was less mighty than my mind
Had dreamed of. Since I could not boast of strength
Great as I wished, weakness was all my boast.
I sought yet hated pity till at length
I earned it. Oh, too heavy was the cost.
But now that there is something I could use
My youth and strength for, I deny the age,
The care and weakness that I know—refuse
To admit I am unworthy of the wage
Paid to a man who gives up eyes and breath
For what can neither ask nor heed his death.

The Green Roads

The green roads that end in the forest
Are strewn with white goose feathers this June,

Like marks left behind by some one gone to the forest
To show his track. But he has never come back.

Down each green road a cottage looks at the forest.
Round one the nettle towers; two are bathed in flowers.

An old man along the green road to the forest
Strays from me, from another a child alone.

In the thicket bordering the forest,
All day long a thrush twiddles his song.

It is old, but the trees are young in the forest,
All but one like a castle keep, in the middle deep.

That oak saw the ages pass in the forest:
They were a host, but their memories are lost,

For the tree is dead: all things forget the forest
Excepting perhaps me, when now I see

The old man, the child, the goose feathers at the edge of the
      forest,
And hear all day long the thrush repeat his song.

When First

When first I came here I had hope,
Hope for I knew not what. Fast beat
My heart at sight of the tall slope
Of grass and yews, as if my feet

Only by scaling its steps of chalk
Would see something no other hill
Ever disclosed. And now I walk
Down it the last time. Never will

My heart beat so again at sight
Of any hill although as fair
And loftier. For infinite
The change, late unperceived, this year,

The twelfth, suddenly, shows me plain.
Hope now,—not health, nor cheerfulness,
Since they can come and go again,
As often one brief hour witnesses,—

Just hope has gone for ever. Perhaps
I may love other hills yet more
Than this: the future and the maps
Hide something I was waiting for.

One thing I know, that love with chance
And use and time and necessity
Will grow, and louder the heart's dance
At parting than at meeting be.

The Gallows

There was a weasel lived in the sun
With all his family,
Till the keeper shot him with his gun
And hung him up on a tree,
Where he swings in the wind and rain,
In the sun and in the snow,
Without pleasure, without pain,
On the dead oak tree bough.

There was a crow who was no sleeper,
But a thief and a murderer
Till a very late hour; and this keeper
Made him one of the things that were,
To hang and flap in rain and wind,
In the sun and in the snow.
There are no more sins to be sinned
On the dead oak tree bough.

There was a magpie, too,
Had a long tongue and a long tail;
He could both talk and do—
But what did that avail?
He, too, flaps in the wind and rain
Alongside weasel and crow,
Without pleasure, without pain,
On the dead oak tree bough.

And many other beasts
And birds, skin, bone and feather,
Have been taken from their feasts
And hung up there together,
To swing and have endless leisure
In the sun and in the snow,
Without pain, without pleasure,
On the dead oak tree bough.

The Dark Forest

Dark is the forest and deep, and overhead
Hang stars like seeds of light
In vain, though not since they were sown was bred
Anything more bright.

And evermore mighty multitudes ride
About, nor enter in;
Of the other multitudes that dwell inside
Never yet was one seen.

The forest foxglove is purple, the marguerite
Outside is gold and white,
Nor can those that pluck either blossom greet
The others, day or night.

When He Should Laugh

When he should laugh the wise man knows full well:
For he knows what is truly laughable.
But wiser is the man who laughs also,
Or holds his laughter, when the foolish do.

How at Once

How at once should I know,
When stretched in the harvest blue
I saw the swift's black bow,
That I would not have that view
Another day
Until next May
Again it is due?

The same year after year—
But with the swift alone.
With other things I but fear
That they will be over and done
Suddenly
And I only see
Them to know them gone.

Gone, Gone Again

Gone, gone again,
May, June, July,
And August gone,
Again gone by.

Not memorable
Save that I saw them go,
As past the empty quays
The rivers flow.

And now again,
In the harvest rain,
The Blenheim oranges
Fall grubby from the trees,

As when I was young—
And when the lost one was here—
And when the war began
To turn young men to dung.

Look at the old house,
Outmoded, dignified,
Dark and untenanted,
With grass growing instead

Of the footsteps of life,
The friendliness, the strife;
In its beds have lain
Youth, love, age and pain:

I am something like that;
Only I am not dead,
Still breathing and interested
In the house that is not dark:—

I am something like that:
Not one pane to reflect the sun,
For the schoolboys to throw at—
They have broken every one.

That Girl's Clear Eyes

That girl's clear eyes utterly concealed all
Except that there was something to reveal.
And what did mine say in the interval?
No more: no less. They are but as a seal
Not to be broken till after I am dead;
And then vainly. Every one of us
This morning at our tasks left nothing said,
In spite of many words. We were sealed thus,
Like tombs. Nor until now could I admit
That all I cared for was the pleasure and pain
I tasted in the stony square sunlit,
Or the dark cloisters, or shade of airy plane,
While music blazed and children, line after line,
Marched past, hiding the "Seventeen Thirty-Nine."

What Will They Do?

What will they do when I am gone? It is plain
That they will do without me as the rain
Can do without the flowers and the grass
That profit by it and must perish without.
I have but seen them in the loud street pass;
And I was naught to them. I turned about
To see them disappearing carelessly.
But what if I in them as they in me
Nourished what has great value and no price?
Almost I thought that rain thirsts for a draught
Which only in the blossom's chalice lies,
Until that one turned back and lightly laughed.

The Trumpet

Rise up, rise up,
And, as the trumpet blowing
Chases the dreams of men,
As the dawn glowing
The stars that left unlit
The land and water,
Rise up and scatter
The dew that covers
The print of last night's lovers—
Scatter it, scatter it!

While you are listening
To the clear horn,
Forget, men, everything
On this earth newborn,
Except that it is lovelier
Than any mysteries.
Open your eyes to the air
That has washed the eyes of the stars
Through all the dewy night:
Up with the light,
To the old wars;
Arise, arise!

The Child in the Orchard

"He rolls in the orchard: he is stained with moss
And with earth, the solitary old white horse.
Where is his father and where is his mother
Among all the brown horses? Has he a brother?
I know the swallow, the hawk, and the hern;
But there are two million things for me to learn.

"Who was the lady that rode the white horse
With rings and bells to Banbury Cross?
Was there no other lady in England beside
That a nursery rhyme could take for a ride?
The swift, the swallow, the hawk, and the hern.
There are two million things for me to learn.

"Was there a man once who straddled across
The back of the Westbury White Horse
Over there on Salisbury Plain's green wall?
Was he bound for Westbury, or had he a fall?
The swift, the swallow, the hawk, and the hern.
There are two million things for me to learn.

"Out of all the white horses I know three,
At the age of six; and it seems to me
There is so much to learn, for men,
That I dare not go to bed again.
The swift, the swallow, the hawk, and the hern.
There are millions of things for me to learn."

Lights Out

I have come to the borders of sleep,
The unfathomable deep
Forest, where all must lose
Their way, however straight
Or winding, soon or late;
They can not choose.

Many a road and track
That since the dawn's first crack
Up to the forest brink
Deceived the travellers,
Suddenly now blurs,
And in they sink.

Here love ends—
Despair, ambition ends;
All pleasure and all trouble,
Although most sweet or bitter,
Here ends, in sleep that is sweeter
Than tasks most noble.

There is not any book
Or face of dearest look
That I would not turn from now
To go into the unknown
I must enter, and leave, alone,
I know not how.

The tall forest towers:
Its cloudy foliage lowers
Ahead, shelf above shelf:
Its silence I hear and obey
That I may lose my way
And myself.

The Long Small Room

The long small room that showed willows in the west
Narrowed up to the end the fireplace filled,
Although not wide. I liked it. No one guessed
What need or accident made them so build.

Only the moon, the mouse and the sparrow peeped
In from the ivy round the casement thick.
Of all they saw and heard there they shall keep
The tale for the old ivy and the older brick.

When I look back I am like moon, sparrow and mouse
That witnessed what they could never understand
Or alter or prevent in the dark house.
One thing remains the same—this my right hand

Crawling crab-like over the clean white page,
Resting awhile each morning on the pillow,
Then once more starting to crawl on towards age.
The hundred last leaves stream upon the willow.

The Sheiling

It stands alone
Up in a land of stone
All worn like ancient stairs,
A land of rocks and trees
Nourished on wind and stone.

And all within
Long delicate has been;
By arts and kindliness
Coloured, sweetened, and warmed
For many years has been.

Safe resting there
Men hear in the travelling air
But music, pictures see
In the same daily land
Painted by the wild air.

One maker's mind
Made both, and the house is kind
To the land that gave it peace,
And the stone has taken the house
To its cold heart and is kind.

The Lane

Some day, I think, there will be people enough
In Froxfield to pick all the blackberries
Out of the hedges of Green Lane, the straight
Broad lane where now September hides herself
In bracken and blackberry, harebell and dwarf gorse.
Today, where yesterday a hundred sheep
Were nibbling, halcyon bells shake to the sway
Of waters that no vessel ever sailed . . .
It is a kind of spring: the chaffinch tries
His song. For heat it is like summer too.
This might be winter's quiet. While the glint
Of hollies dark in the swollen hedges lasts—
One mile—and those bells ring, little I know
Or heed if time be still the same, until
The lane ends and once more all is the same.

Out in the Dark

Out in the dark over the snow
The fallow fawns invisible go
With the fallow doe;
And the winds blow
Fast as the stars are slow.

Stealthily the dark haunts round
And, when a lamp goes, without sound
At a swifter bound
Than the swiftest hound,
Arrives, and all else is drowned;

And I and star and wind and deer
Are in the dark together,—near,
Yet far,—and fear
Drums on my ear
In that sage company drear.

How weak and little is the light,
All the universe of sight,
Love and delight,
Before the might,
If you love it not, of night.

Last Poem

The sorrow of true love is a great sorrow
And true love parting blackens a bright morrow:
Yet almost they equal joys, since their despair
Is but hope blinded by its tears, and clear
Above the storm the heavens wait to be seen.
But greater sorrow from less love has been
That can mistake lack of despair for hope
And knows not tempest and the perfect scope
Of summer, but a frozen drizzle perpetual
Of drops that from remorse and pity fall
And cannot ever shine in the sun or thaw,
Removed eternally from the sun's law.

13.1.17